Joseph Guarnerius, His Work and His Master [Andreas Gisalberti]

JOSEPH GUARNERIUS,
HIS WORK AND HIS MASTER.

PRINTED BY E. SHORE AND CO.,
3, GREEN TERRACE, ROSEBERY AVENUE, LONDON, E.C.

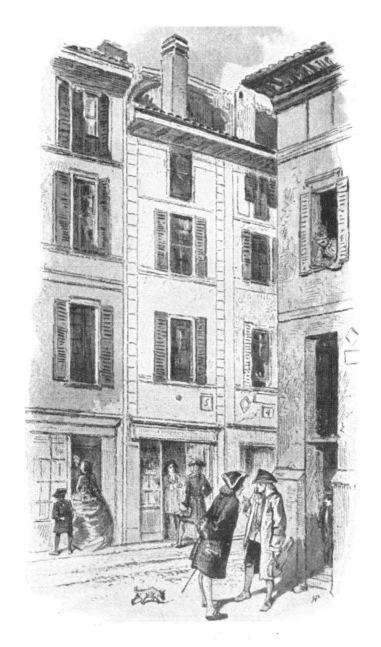

THE HOUSE OF JOSEPH GUARNERIUS.

JOSEPH GUARNERIUS,

HIS WORK AND HIS MASTER.

BY

HORACE PETHERICK,

*Of the Music Jury, International Inventions Exhibition,
South Kensington, 1885; International Exhibition,
Edinburgh, 1890; Expert in Law Courts, 1891;
President of the Cremona Society.*

WITH NUMEROUS ILLUSTRATIONS BY THE AUTHOR
AND
41 FULL-PAGE REPRODUCTIONS OF PHOTOGRAPHS.

London
"THE STEAD" OFFICE, CLESS TERRACE, ROSEBERY AVENUE, E.C.
J. LENG & CO., FLEET STREET, E.C.
New York:
CHARLES SCRIBNER'S SONS, 153-157, FIFTH AVENUE.
1906.

THE HOUSE OF JOSEPH GUARNERIUS.

"THE STRAD" LIBRARY, No. XVI.

JOSEPH GUARNERIUS,

HIS WORK AND HIS MASTER.

BY

HORACE PETHERICK,

*Of the Music Jury, International Inventions Exhibition,
South Kensington, 1885; International Exhibition,
Edinburgh, 1890; Expert in Law Courts, 1891;
- President of the Cremona Society.*

WITH NUMEROUS ILLUSTRATIONS BY THE AUTHOR
AND
41 FULL-PAGE REPRODUCTIONS OF PHOTOGRAPHS.

London:

"THE STRAD" Office, 3, Green Terrace, Rosebery Avenue, E.C.
J. LENG & Co., 186, Fleet Street, E.C.

New York:

CHARLES SCRIBNER'S SONS, 153-157, Fifth Avenue.

1906.

PREFATORY REMARKS.

THE name of the great Italian violin maker Joseph Guarnerius, or as he would have been locally in his native city, Giuseppe Guarneri, the rival, in modern estimation, of the renowned Antonio Stradivari, has for long, always it might almost be said, had a peculiar fascination for the devotees of the art of violin playing, inasmuch as in distinction from the known gradual methodical prosaic progress from youth to patriarchal age of the master who was by many decades his senior, there has been much of romance and mystery surrounding the little that has been handed down concerning his working career, his relationships and even his end. Tradition, what there is of it concerning him, has been much distorted to suit the fancies or promptings of desire in the minds of his would-be biographers. That there is so little of reliable information concerning the great liutaro besides others of his craft in Italy is in consonance with the peacefulness and privacy of their art, and which at the time would have been scarcely noticeable outside the comparatively narrow circle of interested people with whom they were in contact. While they with their contemporaries, assistants or followers were working day by day, content with the remuneration for their labour which the value of it at the time permitted, there was nothing perceptible, it may be safely asserted, that would suggest any probable cessation in the output of the high order of musical stringed instruments for which their city had been for so long renowned.

Without doubt appearances pointed to the probabilities of the requirements continuing to the full extent and that the law of demand and supply would work steadily as hitherto, that pupils would arise and take the places vacated by their masters, and so continue the practice of the art on the same lines during future generations.

This evenness of progress was not destined to continue, the presiding muse having made a lengthy stay was about to gradually withdraw her favours, to vanish and possibly reappear in the far future, but where and when no one can foretell.

There seems to have been a lull or pause after the disappearance of the group of masters, the praise of whom has since made the whole world ring. Other men rose in turn and gave faint promise of filling up the gap that seemed to be opening wider and wider as time progressed, till at last it dawned upon the minds of observers that there was no sign apparent on the horizon that the art would again be what it was in former times, in short it had departed.

The connoisseurs now began collecting, and dealers to make money out of them. The outside world wanted what was increasingly difficult to obtain, and so fraudulent imitators did their best to deceive all. The public interest in the old, now great, masters grew yearly, and inquiries were on foot as to the kind of men they were, how they lived, what they did, besides any possible intelligence concerning their manners, customs, virtues and vices, of which as a whole there was scarcely more than a few idle stories. The circumscribed little world in which they moved was undergoing a change which perhaps seemed gradual during its progress, but was, as we now look back upon it, somewhat rapid and not slow.

This change, however, was a substantial and permanent one ; whether commencing at the chief centres of the art or closing in upon them from surrounding countries, is a question that may well be taken up for attention in the future. At present we can only take the circumstances as they present themselves and consider the main features in connection therewith, the principal being the gradual elbowing out of the field of the old type of liutaros and the substitution of the modern manufacturer with his middleman or agent. To-day he is to be recognized in a palatial residence on the side of a hill while his factory hands are in the most modest of dwelling-houses below, used by divided and subdivided groups of workers in which are included women and children, each taking their part and keeping to that solely. Thus each detail is completed swiftly and cheaply as possible, the finished—can we say harmonious--structure being exported not by parcels of ten or twenty but many thousands every year.

This speaks loudly concerning the growing requirements of musical people in most parts of the world.

As the process of manufacturing grew in years and quantity, the fact of the diminution in numbers of the works of the old type of Italian liutaros was impressing itself more strongly than ever, the best known names among the old Italian masters were on the lips of all who were interested in the acquisition of good instruments, works by their presumed pupils which bore any supposed resemblance to those of their instructor were soon relieved of their labels and put forward as by the master himself ; when these were not obtainable the inevitable close copy or forgery took the place.

Thus as time moved onward the works of masters in the different working centres of the old art rose and are still rising in value, the desire for possessing violins with the magic of a great name attached thereto being intensified, a large number of makers known in their own day as of the first class were, one after another, relegated to the shades of oblivion.

Thus, among others that may yet come forward again for public recognition was a name, Andreas Gisalberti, that in the following pages will, for the first time, be placed before readers of our day as a maker of renown, and for long, until recently, among the large army of forgotten ones, yet judging from circumstances in connection with what of his work is at present known, besides the association of his name with Joseph Guarnerius as his teacher, he must have been recognised in his own day as fairly prominent among the brethren of his craft.

At present his works may be said to be very rare, but when his name begins to be handed about again and attention drawn to it in different parts of Europe, there is every likelihood many will emerge from this obscurity and receive adequate recognition of their merits.

CONTENTS.

CHAPTER I.   PAGE.

Coincidences in the Fine Arts at Various Times and Places
—Rise of the Science and Art of Music—The Invention
of the Violin and its Progress as a Work of Art—The
Masters at Different Working Centres   1

CHAPTER II.

The Styles and Peculiarities of the Works in Various
Localities, Qualities of Tone and other Distinguishing
Characteristics—The Brescian and Cremonese School
and Offshoots   7

CHAPTER III.

The Future Rival of Stradivari, from whence he came—The
high Estimation in which Stradivari was held by the
Liutaros of his Neighbourhood—The Amatis, Guarneris
and Ruggeris—Masters lost sight of—The Name of
Andreas Gisalberti reappears as a Wandering Liutaro..   11

CHAPTER IV.

Andreas Gisalberti *alias* Sante Ballarini, his Varnish,
Modelling and Materials—His Tone   22

CHAPTER V.

Many Masterpieces Lost, their Identity Removed in Order to
substitute other Names for them—Gisalberti's Numerous
Types at Different Localities—His Gifted Pupil at
Cremona—Birth and Family Connections—Reference to
same in Various Books   33

CHAPTER VI.

Joseph Guarnerius's First Appearance—Early Work and
Tickets—His Contemporaries—The Condition of the Art
in Cremona at the Time—The precise Position of his
First Atelier not Known—Joseph's First Tickets in his
Violins—Fulfilling the Requirement of the Hour—Modi-
fications in his Designs—His Wood and Varnish—His
Mode of Affixing the Neck   44

CHAPTER VII.

Of Thicknesses—The Sizes of the Violins by Joseph and his
Teacher—The Tuition of Gisalberti, who is said to have
married into the Mariani Family—Many of his Works
probably still Extant but Undiscovered   59

CONTENTS.

CHAPTER VIII.   PAGE.

Joseph's Peculiarity of Handiwork in Detail, the Modelling,
$f f$, and the Nicks—His and His Teacher's Heads, with
the Volutes or Turns—The Free Gouging of Them—The
Peg Box—Height of Ribs   72

CHAPTER IX.

Further Reference to the Tickets of Gisalberti when he was
staying at Bozzolo—His Violins made to suit his Patrons
there—His Wood and Interior Work—The Occasional
Confusion of Joseph with Gisalberti—The Tone Peculiarities of Either—Different Places where Gisalberti
Worked—His Making of Violoncellos   79

CHAPTER X.

The Pine Used by the Old Italian Makers—Its Peculiarities
and Tone-Producing Qualities—The Storage of Timber
by the Many Makers—Worm-Punctured Wood   96

CHAPTER XI.

Joseph's Efforts at Improvement in Design—His Ideal Care-
fully Sought After—Working on the Lines of Simplicity
—The Tuition of the Cremonese Masters—Were any
Self-Taught ?—The Teaching of Gisalberti Thrown Aside
by Joseph—Peculiarities of Modelling Introduced from
Time to Time — Changes in Varnish — Increase of
Intensity of Colour—Alteration in System of Linings—
Interior Finish of Different Makers—Difference Between
that of Joseph and Stradivari—Effective Appearance ..   108

CHAPTER XII.

Probable Reasons for the Small Pegs Inserted on the Back
and Front by Different Liutaros—Further Modification
of the ff—The Angles of the Ribs—Manner of Securing
the Neck—Different Touches over the Scroll—The
House of Guarneri, Andrea Guarneri, and his sons
Joseph and Peter—Peter Guarnerius of Venice—Relationship of the two Josephs—Their Working Together—The
Border—Further Remarks on the Gouging of Scrolls
by Joseph I.H.S.   124

CHAPTER XIII.

Stradivari and the two Josephs—Joseph I.H.S. and His
Customers—Old Antonio and the Church of S. Domenico
—The Proximity of Carlo Bergonzi and his Two Sons—
The Ruggieris and Others—The Interior of Joseph's
House, His Working Apartment—His Store of Wood—
The Sizes of His Violins   141

CHAPTER XIV.

Joseph's Masterpieces in his Prime, when he was in Posses-
sion of all Necessary Means for their Production—His
Teacher Still Alive with a Nickname—Joseph Taking
Hints from the Works of Others—Mistakes about Joseph
Working with Stradivari : how Caused—The Greatest
of Scroll Carvers—Reference to the Different *ff* of
Joseph—Joseph Continuing the Business on the Decease
of his Cousin—Other Masters Altered to Pass as Joseph's
Work ; Curious Frauds—Adaptations of Details by
Masters from other Works—The Varied *ff* of G. P.
Maggini 150

PAGE.

CHAPTER XV.

The Low Modelling of Joseph not Entirely his Introduction
—The Long Waisted Josephs—The Period 1730-40—
Francesco Stradivari—The now Exploded Story of
Joseph's Idle Life, etc.—Carlo Bergonzi's Imitation of
the Style of Joseph's Hasty Work—The Makers whose
Work has Passed as " Prison Josephs"—Efforts at the
Time to Obtain Joseph's Tone Quality—Joseph's Varia-
tions in Design and Execution—Further Remarks on
Joseph's Scroll Variations—The Treatment of the Ribs
by Him—His Use of Salice for Linings—Some Particu-
lars of Well-Preserved Instruments—Joseph's Bar, His
Fingerboards and Tailpieces 171

CHAPTER XVI.

Joseph's most Finished Period—His Flattest Modelling, His
Refinement—The Gorgeousness of some Specimens—
Joseph's Free Style at its Height—His Purfling at Times
—His Purfling Tool 191

CHAPTER XVII.

Joseph's Late Varnish and that of his Contemporaries in
other Places, Difference between it and his Earlier Kind
—The Decadence of the Italian Varnishes Generally—
Their Peculiarities and Differences of Material—His
Sycamore Bored by Insects—His Effort to Save and not
Throw Away his Work 203

CHAPTER XVIII.

Whether Joseph Made many Violas—One with the Lady's
Name as Maker—The Mysterious I.H.S. Solved—General
Review of Joseph's Working Career 215

LIST OF PLATES.

PLATE I.—Violin, Andreas Gisalberti, c. 1700-5, front view
,, II.—   ,,   ,,   ,,   ,,   back ,,
,, III.—   ,,   ,,   ,,   ,,   side ,,
,, IV.—Scroll of ditto ...   .   front view
,, V.—   ,,   ,, ...   back ,,
,, VI.—   ,,   ,, ...   side ,,

Plates 1 to 6 inserted after page 16.

PLATE VII.—Violin, Sante Ballarini, Andreas Gisalberti,
                    c. 1725-34 ...   .   front view
,, VIII.—Violin, Sante Ballarini, Andreas Gisalberti,
                    c. 1725-34 ...   .   back view
,,   IX.—Violin, Sante Ballarini, Andreas Gisalberti,
                    c. 1725-34 ...   .   side view

Plates 7 to 9 inserted after page 32.

PLATE X.—Violin, Joseph Guarnerius, c. 1706, front view
,, XI.—   ,,   ,,   ,,   ,,   back ,,
,, XII.—   ,,   ,,   ,,   ,,   side ,,

Plates 10 to 12 inserted after page 48.

PLATE XIII.—Violin, Joseph   Guarnerius c. 1710-3,
                                                    front view
,,   XIV.—   ,,   ,,   ,,   back ,,
,,   XV.—   ,,   ,,   ,,   side ,,

Plates 13 to 15 inserted after page 64.

PLATE XVI.—Viola, Andreas   Gisalberti,   Rimini,
                    c. 1720-5   ...   . front view
,, XVII.—Viola,   Andreas   Gisalberti,   Rimini,
                    c. 1720-5   ...   . back view

LIST OF PLATES.

PLATE XVIII.—Violoncello, Andreas Gisalberti, c. 1716,
                                                    front view
  „   XIX.—   „   „   „   back „
  „   XX.—Scroll of ditto   ...   ... front view
  „   XXI.—   „   „   ...   ... back „
  „   XXII.—   „   „   ...   ... side „
  „ XXIII.—Violin, Joseph Guarnerius, c.1710, front „
  „ XXIV.—   „   „   „   „ back „
  „   XXV.—   „   „   „   „ side „

Plates 16 to 25 inserted after page 96.

PLATE XXVI.—Violin, Joseph Guarnerius, c. 1720,
                                                    front view
  „ XXVII.—   „   „   „ back „
  „XXVIII.—Scroll of ditto   ...   ... front view
  „ XXIX.—   „   „   ...   ... back „
  „   XXX.—   „   „   ...   ... side „

Plates 26 to 30 inserted after page 144.

PLATE XXXI.—Violin, Joseph Guarnerius, c. 1735,
                                                    front view
  „ XXXII.—   „   „   „ back „
  „XXXIII.—Violin, Joseph Guarnerius, c. 1730,
                                                    front view
  „ XXXIV.—   „   „   „ back view
  „ XXXV.—   „   „   „ side „

Plates 31 to 35 inserted after page 160.

PLATE XXXVI.—Violin, Joseph Guarnerius, c. 1740,
                                                    front view
  „ XXXVII.—   „   „   „ back „
  „ XXXVIII.—Scroll of ditto „   „   front „
  „ XXXIX.— „   „   ...   ... back „
  „   XL.—   „   „   ...   ... side „

Plates 36 to 40 inserted after page 192.

PLATE XLI.—The House of Joseph Guarnerius ...
                                                    Frontispiece.

JOSEPH GUARNERIUS:

HIS WORK AND HIS MASTER.

CHAPTER I.

COINCIDENCES IN THE FINE ARTS AT VARIOUS TIMES AND
PLACES—RISE OF THE SCIENCE AND ART OF MUSIC
—THE INVENTION OF THE VIOLIN AND ITS PROGRESS
AS A WORK OF ART—THE MASTERS AT DIFFERENT
WORKING CENTRES.

IT is more than a little remarkable that in connection
with the sister arts and sciences of music, painting,
sculpture, and literature,—these not all nor confined
to one place,—the great masters who by the world's
verdict take precedence and tower above all their fellows,
go by twos and twos.

Pictured in the minds of their admirers they are rivals,
notwithstanding that they may never have known each
other personally, or may not have been contemporaneous
in the strictest sense of the term.

As illustrations we may trace far back in the historical
records of the world's most famous men the names of
Apelles, Phaedias, Socrates and Plato of ancient Greece,
noting on our way upwards the luminaries of the Renaissance, Titian and Tintoretto among the Venetian, with
Raphael and Michael Angelo of the Florentine school of
painters. Nearer to our own time come the great
masters of melody and harmony, George Frederick
Handel and Sebastian Bach, followed no long time after
by Mozart and Beethoven.

Whether the coincidences be apparent only, and the

B

outcome, simply, of the classifying tendency in the mind of man in the endeavours to discriminate between the good, bad, and indifferent, or whether during intellectual evolution "the force of nature" exerts itself in a final effort at reaching the point of culmination in producing the best of its kind, we may leave for the researches of psychological students; we have here to call attention to the facts only.

Of all sciences, that of music, as we now understand it, may fairly be said to have been latest in its development, if not altogether begotten of thought in comparatively recent times.

Music among the ancients was—so far as data within our grasp will allow us to judge—a sensuous addition or help only to the outward expression of the emotions stirred or excited by current events.

It was not till the fifteenth century that the science of music, in the modern sense of the term, began to develop and give indication of what was to follow in those succeeding.

At the end of the sixteenth the means of practically demonstrating the extension of musical ideas was notably accompanied by the introduction of the violin.

It came as a simple, yet complete instrument from the hands of an Italian of superlative genius, Gasparo Bertolotis, more generally known among violin players since his time as Gasparo da Salo, who worked at the construction of the then new kind of instrument in the city of Brescia for many years.

After his decease the fabrication was continued by his pupils and followers, who had, as time went on, separated into distinct schools and originated different styles of workmanship and individualities of tone.

The violin by this time was universally recognised as an instrument possessing dual functions, that of pleasing the cultured in the properties of artistic fine design, form, and colour, while sustaining its position as an instrument of exceptional character and potent help in the onward march of musical art.

Naturally enough, during the contest for patronage among the different members of the various schools or centres then cropping up all over Italy, there would arise men of exceptional talent and capacity for the art which they had chosen as their means of livelihood; born and bred apparently specially for the chosen work, as the saying is, when their productions still extant are scrutinised.

The men or masters, as the moderns term them, were endowed to an amazing extent by nature with that keen perception of what was beautiful and attractive to the eye, and which they were careful to implant in all the productions of their hands.

It was sometimes chiefly confined to the general aspect, close attention to minute details being apparently neglected or deemed as but inferior adjuncts to the excellence of the whole work. At others, supreme attention seems to have been centred on the production of a work matchless in mechanical neatness, delicacy and grace of form, with beauty of colour such as ancient Greece or renascent Italy alone has as yet put before the searching, covetous eye of the connoisseur in all civilised countries.

It was to the ranks of such artists, the term being understood in its most comprehensive sense, that the members of the renowned Amati family of Cremona, who with Giovanni Paolo Maggini were the immediate successors of Gasparo Bertolotis, belonged.

Their first efforts were directed towards the attainment of a higher grade in the construction and finish of the violin, above what was possibly looked upon at the time and locally as sufficiently good for ordinary requirements. But men of their constitution and refined perceptions were not likely to remain long on uncultivated ground, when a whole vista presented itself before their widening mental vision, in which the ideal seemed present of almost every variety of work upon which they had hitherto placed their hands.

To the possibilities in the future their energies were directed by regular degrees and with singleness of aim, the goal of their ambition was the attainment of the greatest possible excellence in every part, in order that the totality should be beyond compare.

The wonderful Amati family were not alone while working on these lines; in company with them the Ruggeris tried to keep pace, but did not possess equal powers of originality. Quite as numerous as the Amatis, they were prolifically perhaps ahead of them : they also had, as it were, "hanging on to the skirts of their garments," many trying to do as they did, with occasional success in a modified way.

These, from a variety of causes, some of which they may even have combated and failed, went to other places and became in themselves fresh sources of supply for the growing needs of the musical world.

With the Amatis and Ruggeris in the city of Cremona, many liutaros were working side by side. Some, whose names alone have been handed down to us, may have won a degree of celebrity during their day in the comparatively narrow confines of their own circle of patronage. Others may not have lived long enough to secure a recognised standing among the yet extending ranks of the Cremonese school.

Owing to these, and most likely many other circumstances occurring at the time and since, not forgetting the removal from the interior of the original labels, a large number of instruments, some of a high standard of excellence, are floating about in different parts of the world, the authorship of which no one can point to with any degree of certainty.

A somewhat peculiar phase of the liutaro's art in Italy was the frequency with which the calling was continued for several generations, the son, grandson, or great grandson following each other in regular rotation, with perhaps a relative or two of the same name.

Among the many instances besides the families of Amati and Ruggeri was that of the Guarneri, whose progenitor was trained in the house of the first-mentioned, or it may be said "took his degree" there.

There can be no mistake that in estimating the position of the Amatis, they are found to have occupied a position of the highest importance in the practice of an art then generally recognised over Europe as being a particular Italian speciality, and further, by renown, of the city of Cremona itself. The mention of this name was then, as now, synonymous with a violin of superlative excellence.

The culminating point of the art of Cremona—for that had become the chief settlement of the industry—was not destined to be reached by a member of the Amati family, notwithstanding the fact of the greatest among them having brought the elegance of form, proportion, and finish, to a pitch beyond which there seemed to be no possibility of advance.

Indeed, it must have seemed to thoughtful musicians of the period that the art of producing the combined excellencies was likely to remain at one standard, that which had been hitherto maintained with such masterful and unrivalled ability for generations.

This was not to be so, however ; notwithstanding the fact of the greatest genius of the Amati family being one of the latest, and he moreover proving the possibility of going a step further on the same lines, the highest degree had not yet been reached. This was not destined to be accomplished by one of the family in name or blood relationship ; it was to be a continued development of their genius in a sense no less true or direct in the person of their greatest pupil, Antonio Stradivari, whose work of hand so early in his career gave evidence of that personal and careful training, of the kind which the great masters of other arts are known to have received and then transmitted in turn to younger ones.

But while this lineal descent of the highest qualities of the art of violin making at Cremona seemed likely to be continuous, the name of the place having in foreign countries as well as locally become synonymous in the musical world with that of a fine violin, there were branches and off-shoots also from the famous centre of the art. Pupils had departed into different cities, with the principles imbibed at the fountain-head carefully stored in their minds, and which, under fresh circumstances and with different materials within reach, they were to make practical and meet the requirements of the different localities in which they had determined to settle.

Thus we find that many pupils of the Amatis who were carrying the excellencies of the Cremonese into fresh districts of Italy, gave the impress of their own individuality to the products of their industry, bringing forth fresh styles or founding new schools. As instances of this the Milanese, with Paolo Grancino, the Neapolitans with Alexander Gagliano, the Tyrolese with Jacob Stainer, besides others at Venice and places of lesser importance, may be noted.

Each of these, from either their individual fancies, the requirements of the particular place and people, or the virtues of the materials to be obtained there, found themselves, as the art was spreading abroad, the head or centre of a school or style with which the place was identified.

This brings us to the consideration of the progress of the art from its foundation in the city of Brescia, at the latter part of the sixteenth century.

CHAPTER II.

The Styles and Peculiarities of the Works in Various Localities, Qualities of Tone and other Distinguishing Characteristics — The Brescian and Cremonese School and Offshoots.

ATTENTION diligently applied to the subject of the rise and continuation for more or less time of the various schools, styles or individualities of well-known masters, will necessarily include within it the study of the progress of the peculiarities of tone qualities produced or developed as time went on.

To many people there is little or no interest in the difference between a very old violin of the true Brescian school, and one of a later or Cremonese. It is to some only a question of rank of the maker with the commercial value of his work, to others, the effect likely to be produced by a performer on the particular instrument under their consideration. Attention duly directed to the time, locality and circumstances surrounding the production of these different kinds of excellencies will bring to mind the inexorable law of demand and supply. This soon began to bear upon the production of the then newly introduced musical instrument, the violino of Brescia and Cremona.

It was after the " violino " had become established in Brescia that the demand came from Cremona for the same species, but of a different variety to that in vogue at Brescia. Whether the supply of the requisite quality of tone was offered to or introduced by desire of the dilettanti of Cremona is not recorded. We have the bare fact alone of the Amati family setting up in business there, and sending forth instruments of a different calibre of tone quality. That required by the musical public around was of a lighter character, or it might be termed a more vocal and less organ-like quality than that which the Brescians had been accustomed to.

There was an offshoot of the Brescian school which settled at Pesaro, where its members, headed by Gasparo Boarga d'Archangeli (in all probability a personal pupil of Gasparo da Salo) followed by Antonio Mariani and his sons,—I have been told that there were no less than ten members of the family—became divided among themselves, that is, as regards the tone calibre, some being high, others low.

This, and the Brescian centre itself, lost much of its importance as an influence in the practice of the liutaro's art in Italy ; on the contrary that of Cremona steadily maintained its supremacy, the Amatis, Ruggeris and Guarneris being the best known to foreign buyers at the time.

As observed before, the most eminent of the Amatis, Nicolo, showed that there was possible a step beyond the usual standard of excellence upheld by the rest of the family. This step was in a direction no doubt stimulated, perhaps demanded, by the growth and extension of the dramatic sentiment in musical composition.

To meet this, more energy or intensity of tone was desirable ; the genius of Nicolo Amati was therefore exercised toward the accomplishment of the object.

In this he appears to have been guided by a belief that his predecessors of the same family had gone a trifle too far on one line, while endeavouring to obtain the purest soprano quality, the acme of possibility and the realization of their ideal.

But though his span of life was long, it was not sufficiently so for him to see the full fruition of his labours ; this was reserved for his dearest pupil, Antonio Stradivari, who had been by him duly initiated into all the secrets of his craft which had been handed down from generation to generation.

From the first this wonderful successor of the greatest genius in a family of most extraordinary talent, adhered to the lines worked upon by his great teacher, nor did he swerve from them to the close of a still longer life.

From this view it will be plain that in a measure the old Amati tradition of ways and means to the desired end were cast aside in favour of a slight retrogression towards the nearly defunct Brescian school.

That this return, inconsiderable as it might have seemed, then as now, was accompanied by the much valued additional energy, intensity, and reserve of power—in short the voice of the instrument being enlarged—has been emphatically endorsed by generations of performers and listeners. There seemed to be, in the presence of the masterpieces of workmanship and tone quality associated with the name of Antonio Stradivari, no probability, even remote, of any disturbance of the peaceful occupation of the throne of supremacy by the world famed successor of Nicolo Amati. His pupils or assistants, after being under his flag for a time, departed, implanting it in fresh places or ousting such followers of the Amatis as were content to be mere faint reflections of the principal members of the renowned family.

Was there any possibility at all apparent of a rivalry with such a master of his art as Stradivari of Cremona, he who by the force of comparison might be termed the Raphael, the Shakespeare, the Mozart of his particular art?

Often when nature seems to us to have been on the brink of exhaustion, the reserve forces hidden from our view have proved as boundless as they have been startling.

Notwithstanding the seeming unlikelihood or even impossibility of a rival to the staid monarch of the liutaro's branch of art, yet it was to be, and to come also from an unsuspected direction.

There are two threads to our discourse, the first being

included in the foregoing; the second will call for the
consideration of a maker henceforth of great importance,
in fact he is metaphorically two men squeezed into one,
but that one is not Joseph Guarnerius, I.H.S.

CHAPTER III.

THE FUTURE RIVAL OF STRADIVARI, FROM WHENCE HE
CAME—THE HIGH ESTIMATION IN WHICH STRADIVARI
WAS HELD BY THE LIUTAROS OF HIS NEIGHBOUR-
HOOD—THE AMATIS, GUARNERIS AND RUGGERIS—
MASTERS LOST SIGHT OF—THE NAME OF ANDREAS
GISALBERTI REAPPEARS AS A WANDERING LIUTARO.

THE idea of any possible rivalry with the well-known
maestro who had worked for so many years in the
square of St. Dominic at Cremona, would, in the
minds of his numerous and aristocratic patrons, have been
scouted as most unreasonable and unlikely. Was he not
the acknowledged head of his craft, with all sufficient
patronage, and his name known among kings, nobles and
connoisseurs as a maker to whom preference would be
shown at any time when there might be required the best
quality and most artistically constructed of stringed
instruments? Whence was the rival, if possible, to
spring from? Was he to come from among the numerous
pupils or assistants who, one after another, had been
working, perhaps living, under the same roof with him?

There is some reason in assuming that among those
who had been learning the ways and means of attaining
to the high standard of excellence, artistic as well as
acoustical, that distinguished the house of Stradivari,
there may have been one, if not more, who would, if he
dared, set himself up in both word and deed as being
equal to, or even a degree in advance of, the delimitation
marked out by the Cremonese master.

On the contrary, none of them appear to have been so

disposed; they rather show in all their handiwork the high estimation in which they held their chief, only giving way to their own individuality,—as was quite natural with artists Italian born and bred—while keeping steadily on in the same well appointed road.

The difference conspicuous in the work of any of the known assistants of old Antonio was rather in a falling away from or inability to keep up to the standard than in any determination to make a decided advance in their art.

The whole working career of the master is an exhibition of perfect freedom from the manifestation of any signs of alteration in style or manner, or introduction of any changes that could be assumed to be due to influence from without or admiration of the works of other artists.

Singularly even in its course of development from first to last, his manner of working remained unaffected in every respect, excepting during the inevitable encroachment of old age.

We may therefore conclude from all the details known to us of Stradivari's life and the surrounding circumstances, that so far as he was concerned, during his lifetime there was no rivalry; he became the acknowledged head of the Cremonese art, and retained that position until no longer able to send forth his masterpieces.

Let us now return to the consideration of the Amati school proper. Under this term we will include the many individuals comprised in the Amati and Ruggeri families, some of whom were engaged at Cremona, while others were carrying out the precepts of their teachers at Bologna. Many of their assistants had been working for some time in places of lesser note.

Simultaneously at Cremona the first of the Guarneris, known by his prefix of Andreas, was content to work on the lines of Nicolo Amati, but in a manner more akin to that of Franciscus Ruggeri, for whom, as often as not, he is mistaken. In power of originality he was left some way behind by his two sons, one of whom settled at

Mantua and became great as a maker at that place; the other remained at Cremona, succeeding his father, as his tickets are dated from the same house, with its sign of S. Teresie. Here he made the different kinds of stringed instruments, his energies being particularly directed to the composition of the fine material with which he enveloped his work. As an Italian liutaro of the grand period, he cannot claim a very exalted position with regard to form, his instruments lacking in a degree the quality known as breadth of style. In finish or mechanical neatness he was not ahead of his father.

The Ruggeris were working in close proximity, and probably with a patronage not much below, if not up to, that of other makers of the same school.

It will thus be evident that the Amati principles or theories carried out in the construction and production of tone qualities which distinguish the school were by no means relegated to the background upon the advent of the Stradivarian school, but were still in the front line.

At the time, about 1690 to 1700, the Brescian school may be said to have been nearly extinct; why, is a question wide in its bearings and requiring much erudite research before any prospect of a satisfactory settlement could be discerned.

That emulation prevailed among the individual liutaros of the different cities or even neighbourhoods there cannot be a doubt, and that a spirit of almost antagonism existed between those who were for the Stradivari system and those for the Amati is more than probable, otherwise we should not have found such strict adherence to established methods and styles continuing amongst the partisans for an extended period.

From this it might be argued that men of prominence in the art, practised in different parts, would have had their names handed down to succeeding generations for still greater admiration than they might have been thought deserving of in their own day.

In the consideration of this, however, we must not lose sight of the peculiarities of commerce in those times.

There appears to have been much done in the way of taking the then newly made violins from Cremona, as the chief seat of the art, and selling them in foreign lands, where ready recipients were in waiting for them on account of their pleasing sounding qualities.

Naturally enough, many fine instruments remained in Italy for various reasons, not excluding the requirements of the connoisseurs there; that fine tonal quality among the Italian violins was not invariably accompanied by the exquisite form and finish associated with the name of Amati of Cremona.

Many exquisitely toned violins were left untouched by foreign buyers as unknown and appreciated solely among the musicians of the various localities or near where they were made. They were, many of them, if they escaped the interference of the label traders, to be brought upon the table a generation or two afterwards, when the delicacies of the Amati season were no longer to be had, and the connoisseur's appetite had to be appeased with different fare.

It is therefore no matter for surprise that some masters have only been recognised outside their country long after they had died and were sometimes almost forgotten by their kith and kin in the art.

To one of such our attention is now to be directed.

Of the then, as now known, Amati school—that is chiefly according to tonal considerations—he was doubtless as well or better known to his brethren in the art of Cremona than many whose names have been quite familiar for generations to connoisseurs in the principal cities of Europe.

Although known to but very few people at the present day, his works cannot be said to have been neglected; they have been in use and done good duty as unknown Italians or even occasionally under the title of " Prison Josephs," a convenient appellation when an old Italian violin of rugged outline and good tonal qualities and sufficient mystery in form and colour comes before the dealer.

That this maker was well known at Cremona in his day, that is, at the end of the seventeenth century and the commencement of the eighteenth, will be quite obvious a little further on. He did not reside permanently at Cremona, but shifted about from one place to another. His earliest ticket that I have been able to reproduce is as follows:—

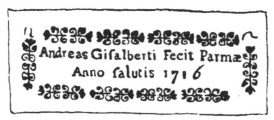

Andreas Gifalberti Fecit Parmæ
Anno falutis 171 6

From the fact of this being a printed ticket, and for which a block must have been made in the way usual among the liutaros of the time, there is great probability that he had been working in Parma for some time. It will thus be seen that in the early years of the eighteenth century, he had, for some reason, changed his residence. In all probability there are still extant many instruments made by him during his sojourn at Cremona, and we may look forward, with some reasonable hope, that a few will be found on discovery to be still intact.

To whom this master, hitherto unknown in this country, owed his early tuition, is a matter that must at present remain as unproven. Neither the work on the outside, nor that in the inside, afford full and satisfactory evidence on which we can form any reasonable hypothesis of his having been trained in Cremona. His patterns, of which he appears to have had many, according to the whim of the moment, are distinct ones, and as unlike anything that we are acquainted with among the Cremonese makers of the period as they are possible to be.

That this has struck many Italian connoisseurs anxious to hang their hobbies and prejudices on some convenient

hook, will be evident when we hear of some having pro-
claimed him to have been a pupil of Giovanni Paolo
Maggini. A reference to the admirable representation
herewith printed of a double purfled violin by Gisalberti
—*(see Plates I., II., and III.)*—will give the reader some
clue to the reasons which have induced some fanciers to
fix upon Maggini as his probable teacher; it is doubtless
the fact of Gisalberti inserting, on occasion, an extra line
of purfling. This, to many enthusiasts in the study of
the subject, would seem a positive indication, being
unaware or oblivious of the fact that double purfling
was a common habit among the Italian makers of different
schools, and was not confined to that of Brescia.

This peculiarity, which, with Gisalberti, may have
appeared on very rare occasions, is the only one which
can be said to have been common to both.

In his general system of modelling, Gisalberti more
nearly approached that of Gasparo da Salo, possibly
from his naturally hasty habit rather than from any
distinct idea of reintroducing the style of the Brescian
master. In the drawing of the curves, there is nothing
in Gisalberti (double purfled) suggestive of Maggini, nor
indeed of Gasparo da Salo; but there is some touch of
the Amati perceptible if we examine the waist curves;
these are effected with much smoothness of contour, but
there is wanting the delicate elaboration or sub-division
of the curving, a branch of art in which the Amati
family exhibited such amazing ability.

There can be very little question as to Gisalberti not
being an adept at the harmonizing of curves by proportion or direction; he seems to have been content to
obtain his effect, upon his stiffer or straighter line above
the upper corners, and below the lower ones.

This peculiarity may be noticed right through his
career; all of his instruments, so far as my knowledge
extends, having this strong mannerism.

Further on it will be found useful to refer again to
this interesting and more carefully manipulated specimen
of Andreas Gisalberti's better class of violin.

Plate I.
VIOLIN, ANDREAS GISALBERTI, C. 1700-5.
Owned by Mr. PHILIP A. ROBSON.

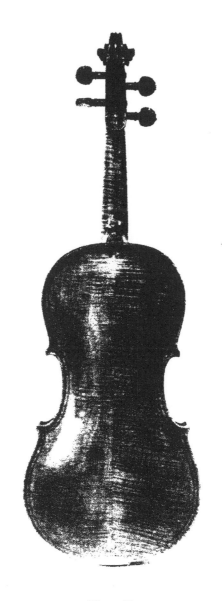

Plate II.
VIOLIN, ANDREAS GISALBERTI, C. 1700-5.
Owned by Mr. PHILIP A. ROBSON.

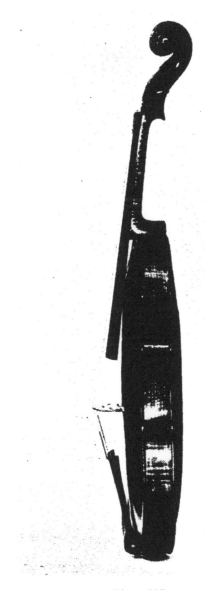

Plate III.
VIOLIN, ANDREAS GISALBERTI, C. 1700-5.
Owned by Mr. PHILIP A. ROBSON.

Plate IV.
VIOLIN, ANDREAS GISALBERTI. SCROLL.

Plate V.
VIOLIN, ANDREAS GISALBERTI. SCROLL.

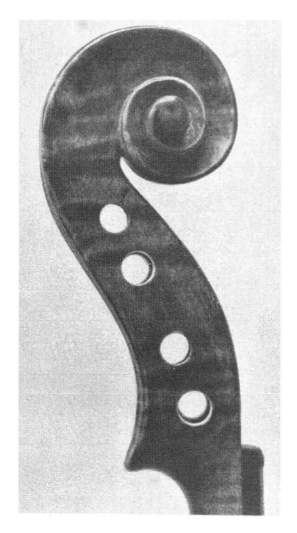

Plate VI.
VIOLIN, ANDREAS GISALBERTI. SCROLL.

Some further peculiarities may be noticed; the border is raised, and in some instances rather sharply. This, as a matter of course, causes the rise of the modelling to appear greater to the eye than is really the case.

Here we have a distinct, if not conclusive, piece of evidence of his belonging not to the old Brescian school at all.

There is sufficient amount of careful finish, however, to have pleased most of the admirers of the Amati system at the time holding such high rank.

Further, we may notice the soundholes; these are the most strikingly peculiar feature of the whole design.

The only maker known to me before the dates of Gisalberti, who used what may be aptly termed the highest developed type of the square-winged soundholes, was Antonio Mariani the elder, of Pesaro, the latest of whose dates I am not acquainted with, so that beyond the resemblance in this matter of details, there is not much to go upon, but if this maker should be found by-and-bye to have been working later than I have hitherto supposed, there will be the continuous chain of makers possibly complete.

We may dispose, once for all, of the Maggini hypothesis, as this master is not heard of after 1636, and therefore to allow of Gisalberti having practised his art under the great Brescian's guidance would have required the concession of a preternaturally long life, Gisalberti working till 1735 or 1740.

Allowing on the other hand the possibility of Gisalberti having been taught by Antonio Mariani, then several details and points of striking resemblance come out with great force.

This quaint old Pesaro liutaro, of whose work I have had before me two, with their original and undisturbed tickets, was working at Pesaro in the year 1666, and he may have continued labouring for some, if not many, years later.

This brings the possibility of Andreas Gisalberti having been a pupil of Antonio Mariani within quite reasonable limits.

C

If this be conceded, there are several other matters in the work of Mariani and Gisalberti that harmonise most satisfactorily. The soundholes of the first, in a specimen that once came under my attention, and of which an illustration is here inserted, will be seen to be very interesting. Next, they were both in possession of the method of compounding most beautiful varnish.

The violin of Mariani's has a striking resemblance to Gisalberti in one of his humours, which will be evident at a glance.

Further, as Antonio Mariani made a distinct departure in the matter of tone calibre after leaving his (I believe) master Maggini, there is nothing surprising in the fact of Gisalberti choosing that of the Amati as the best for presenting himself before the public with an idea of obtaining reputation.

Assuming, then, the connection between the two makers to have been not only possible, but probable, we have the young Gisalberti starting for the famous city of Cremona, where his powers and energies would find full scope.

He took with him, perhaps not a store of wood of proper or suitable acoustic qualities, but the knowledge of where to obtain that which he felt sure would give the tone that would attract attention.

The quality of tone which he brought before the Cremonese world was, although of the Amati calibre, distinct, clear, more voluminous, spreading, refined and soft.

Assuming that he continued working for some years at Cremona, he had, in the year 1716, removed to Parma, where the tickets as before illustrated were issued. We will now leave Andreas Gisalberti at Parma, where he may, or may not, have met with a different measure of success from that achieved at Cremona. Whatever the facts, there can be no doubt of his having exercised considerable influence.

Another name will now engage our attention for a moment or two, more for continuity than from direct necessity.

Some years back, when several researches were in hand, requiring all the spare time and energy at my

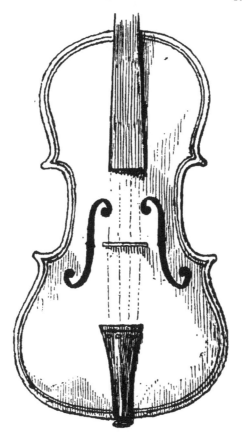

ANTONIO MARIANI, PESARO C. 1660.

DOUBLE PURFLED.

Owned by J. S. Cook, Esq.

command, the violin with the ticket which has been reproduced, was shown me for the first time. After looking over it carefully for some time, I said to the owner, "That is very extraordinary, I have just come into possession of a violin which may be called an actual replica of this."

"Very likely," was the rejoinder, "I have seen others out in Italy also very like them."

"But mine is in excellent preservation, and I am sure the ticket, from surrounding evidence, has never been disturbed ; it has another name, a written one, not printed like yours."

"Just what I should expect," was the reply, "and I tell you the current story in Italy concerning the two names, which will account for the difference. In the first place, the two names belong to one man ; this will account for identicalness in the general appearance, model, and workmanship. Andreas Gisalberti's early work is more carefully executed than his later. It is said the labours of his early period did not bring him in satisfactory remuneration. This may have been the cause of his removal to Parma. Rumour has it that he was a man of some uncertainty in his habits, and being of versatile powers, combined the profession of ballet master (in the evening probably) and violin maker. The manner in which he conducted himself in the ballet master department was such that he acquired the nickname of 'the little ballet saint.' Whether sarcastically meant history does not relate. Being once known by that title, smallness or greatness being thrust upon him, it appears to have settled there, and was accepted by him as the name by which he was to be henceforth popularly known."

It may here be remarked that the nickname appears to have been given to him at Rimini, certainly after his removal there in 1717 from Bozzolo.

It will be seen by the second and third tickets that he had removed to Rimini, which is about eighteen miles north of Pesaro, where, if my hypothesis is correct, he received his first tuition, and that he spent the remainder of his days in his old home of Rimini.

Some of his tickets are here reproduced :—

Sante Ballarini
Fecc.

(Sante Ballarino)
Rimino 1734.

Sancte Ballarini Fᵉ
L'ann 1735 Rimini

CHAPTER IV.

ANDREAS GISALBERTI *alias* SANTE BALLARINI, HIS VARNISH, MODELLING, AND MATERIALS—HIS TONE.

THERE are several particulars of some interest that it will be as well to note concerning the work of Andreas Gisalberti, *alias* Sante Ballarini, before going fully into the consideration of our main subject.

Taking firstly the varnish, that delicate, artistic, and mysterious envelope is, with Gisalberti, of a type distinct among the old Italian liutaros.

It possesses all of the fine qualities that made the varnishes of Cremona and other centres of the art in Italy so world renowned. As a general rule, he did not highly charge it with colour, although he did occasionally use a red.

Its extreme limpidity and freedom from all tendency to hardness is the impression received at the first glance; on the other hand, its constituent materials, aided by his manipulation, appear to have been such that cracks, frizzle, or contracting into wrinkles is not noticeable as with so many of the Venetian school. It is laid on thinly and evenly, almost directly in opposition to what we might have expected to accompany the design and workmanship of his violins. Some of these strike the eye as seemingly drawn in a haphazard manner, but for the presence of some points of detail, which he appears to have always adhered to, and which, doubtless, contribute to the general strength of character. It might even be asserted by critics inclined to hasty generalisation, that he had but little power of drawing.

That this was not actually the case is not very difficult of discernment when the contour of his violins is analytically examined.

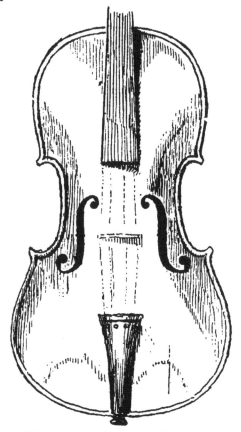

SANTE BALLARINI, ANDREAS GISALBERTI,
RIMINI, 1734.
Owned by John Black, Esq.

Taking as an example the double-purfled specimen already illustrated, we find here that the line above the upper corner is of a formal character inclined to straightness, or somewhat stiff. This is a persistent feature with Gisalberti, and has been present in every instance that has come under my notice, no matter what sort of curve was introduced by way of harmony or contrast at the middle or waist.

The line below the lower corner has the same kind of stiffening, but really equal in this respect with the upper, it is not as evident at first sight owing to the position and larger proportion of the adjacent parts.

Gisalberti's modelling varies, perhaps in accordance with the tastes of his patrons, in the different localities where he worked. When full it is not in the exaggerated or inflated manner of the Stainer copyist, but rather that of the fuller type of Gasparo da Salo when that master was in the humour. Occasionally he made some instruments of decidedly low elevation, such as ought to have pleased the lovers of the " flat model." There appears to me very little room for doubt that if, as is not very improbable, a hunt is once initiated for this most interesting maker, not to say master—a title of which he is quite deserving—it would result in some very attractive specimens being unearthed in out of the way places.

When his characteristics are more fully known to the army of fiddle searchers in England and on the Continent, many instruments hitherto dubbed " unknown Italians," will be recognised as being the work of his hand, and further, having the stamp of his tone. He will then take his rightful position among the known eminent liutaros of Italy. A few further particulars of this maker's work may be interesting and useful for his identification.

His border is mostly rather broad, the rise rather straight or flat from the purfling. The edging, when in iis original condition, is a little over the average in thickness and well rounded. The rather flat dip from the apex, as a matter of course, when meeting at the corners, results in a kind of groove, and when, as is sometimes the case, there is an evidence of haste in the tooling of this part, we have a close resemblance to the kind of indentation supposed to be peculiar to the handiwork of Joseph Guarnerius.

This has not escaped the eye of the peculiar class of dealers anxious to get as much money as possible with the least amount of trouble and time ; the corners have, therefore, when passing through their hands, received their trifling attentions. They have been emphasized, or made to appear, to them, more Joseph like—with increased probability of passing as veritable specimens of his handiwork, and bringing, of course, a proportionately larger sum of money.

There is another peculiarity which Gisalberti seems to have steadfastly adhered to, namely, the treatment of the junction of the ribs at the corners between the upper and lower tables. This is not squared off in the manner practised by so many makers of the Cremonese school, but is left comparatively sharp. This was likewise the habit of Lorenzo Guadagnini, after he had thrown aside the influence of his teacher Stradivari. It would have suggested some connection between the Milanese master and Gisalberti had it not been that in almost every other respect they are in strong disagreement.

Notwithstanding this, however, considering the way in which so many of the Italian liutaros moved about, assisting first one and then the other, there may have been some business connection during the time they were at Cremona ; both makers were young, one possibly taking a hint or being influenced by the other. They may have met and even worked together for a short time, but both men being of very independent mind, neither was likely to borrow much or take many hints from the other.

Another portion of Gisalberti's work and style calls for some attention—that is, respecting the design and execution of the head and scroll. A glance at the photos of the Gisalberti scroll *(See Plates IV., V., VI.)* will be sufficient for perceiving the close affinity in form and workmanship between this specimen and the popularly known types of Joseph Guarnerius.

No wonder that the two makers have been mixed up, sometimes unwittingly, but ofttimes quite the reverse, with an intention to deceive, the likeness being sometimes so close that very few connoisseurs would be keen enough to readily discover the difference.

That there are fine specimens of Joseph Guarnerius now going about with the wrong scrolls, and those having been carved by Andreas Gisalberti, is an assertion that will be readily accepted by those who will make a careful study of the two makers.

The fine varnish on Gisalberti's work, although not strong in colour, would present little difficulty in the eyes of the dealer who thought to make the thing complete, and in such a manner that it would require an expert of equal knowledge with himself to detect the fraud. To him there would only be necessary a slight toning or increase of depth of the top coat of colour.

The manner of gouging and tooling adopted by the two liutaros is also so much alike as to make the deception, so far as it can go, comparatively easy. There is the same deep rugged gouging of the turns, these commencing also at the same point, and the heavy, rather broadly gouged channels at the back down to the shell. The back view, if the connoisseur had been in some little doubt as to the other parts appearing to be the work of Joseph, would tend more towards his conviction that it was really so.

The materials used by Gisalberti are invariably of the best quality, the pine varying, sometimes very close in thread, at others open, and not hard or mechanical.

His sycamore is more often than not of handsome curl, bold and rather regular, inclining downwards each side of the joint; it is cut so as to give due effect to the minute squares, or as they are termed among connoisseurs, "nutmeg" spots. He appears to have had a considerable store of this sycamore, as it appears to be from the same tree that his early as well as his latest instruments are made; or the wood is so similar that he must have had unusual facilities for obtaining it of precisely the same quality and appearance during nearly the whole of his working career.

The interior work of his violins is not of fine finish,

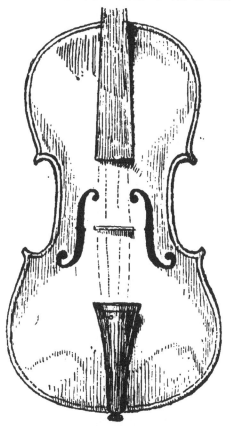

ANDREAS GISALBERTI, SANTE BALLARINI, RIMINI.

the linings are not let into the corner blocks; they are wide and roughly cut to fit against the blocks, these are cut away a little above and below, causing

them to appear octagonal in form when looked at
through the soundholes.

Although the closest examination of Gisalberti's pine
does not enable us to detect any strong points of difference from that of other makers, by which we can obtain
a definite knowledge as to the district or even the
particular province wherein it grew, yet we can fairly
draw our conclusions from other evidence combined with
that of the general appearance, that the trees from which
Gisalberti and his notable pupil, Joseph Guarnerius,
obtained their wood for the upper tables of their violins,
grew in the same latitudes, if not in the exact locality
from which the Amatis drew their supplies.   Briefly, the
evidence is in the peculiarity of the pine from a botanical
aspect, coupled with its acoustic qualities.

If for a moment we turn our attention to the pine used
by the liutaros of the different centres of the art in Italy,
or including those of other countries during the times
under our consideration, we find that the locality of make
is oftentimes indicated by the grain and substance of the
pine, sometimes of the sycamore used, with scarcely the
necessity of referring to the style and workmanship of the
instrument.   Further, with this the individual maker is
often suggested by his very frequent use of a certain
kind of wide or narrow threaded pine.   As an instance,
the two Milanese masters, Lorenzo Guadagnini and Carlo
Ferdinando Landolfi, both favoured an open straight-
threaded pine ; it may have been more adapted to their
requirements, if not less difficult to obtain than a closer-
threaded kind used by makers in other localities.

The variety or quality of pine used by the old Brescian
maker differs from that used by the Cremonese, this
latter differing from that of the makers of Pesaro and of
Genoa, these again differing from the Neapolitan, and all
being distinct from the Tyrolese pine or larch used by
Jacobus Stainer, his pupils and followers.

From this it will be perceived, after a fair study of the
subject, that the makers of a particular school, or sometimes a province or city, sought the kind of tone suitable

to the tastes of their patrons by careful selection from the materials conveniently within reach.

Viewed in this way, Andreas Gisalberti would seem to have concluded, perhaps from observation, if not from

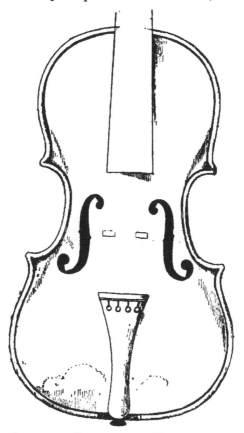

ANDREAS GISALBERTI, PARMA 1716.

suggestions from patrons of his art, that from the source or magazine hitherto worked so successfully by the Amatis, a variety or special kind of tone could be brought forward having a considerably increased volume, while including all the excellencies and attractiveness of that which had been for so long identified with the city of Cremona.

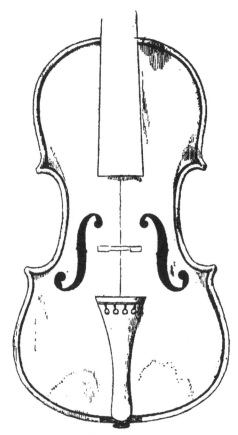

ANDREAS GISALBERTI, C. 1720.

That the production of this tone was not of a haphazard kind, or the thought of a moment, is proved by the persistent production of the identical quality at different periods in his own working career and that of his more famous pupil.

On its introduction among the cognoscenti of Cremona

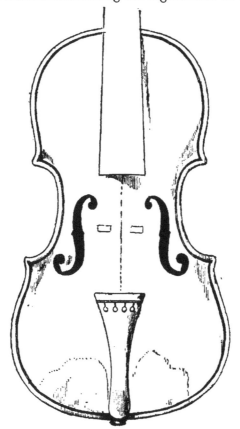

ANDREAS GISALBERTI (SANTE BALLARINI),
1735.

it must have seemed quite an innovation. The public, that of the early part of the eighteenth century (not like the present so occupied with and immersed in an ocean of uncertainty with regard to its appliances and projects for killing distance and time), had been used so long to the dulcet—some would even say infantile—accents of the Amati violins, that Gisalberti may have experienced some uphill work before his innovation was accepted. Be that as it may, there is no room for doubt that he became established for some years at least, and was recognised as a maker of considerable eminence.

The reason for his removal to Parma during or before the year 1716—a comparatively early period in his career —is not, and may never become, known. There is so little in connection with these now acknowledged Italian masters that has been unearthed, that in this particular instance there is scarcely enough on which to hang a vague surmise.

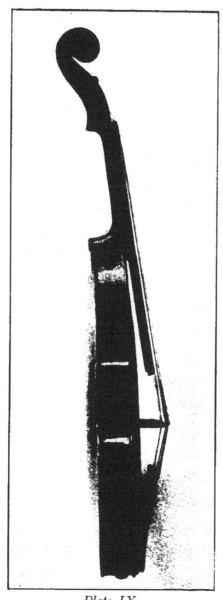

Plate IX.
VIOLIN, SANTE BALLARINI, ANDREAS GISALBERTI,
c. 1725-34.
Owned by Mr. THOS. NESMITH, U.S.A.

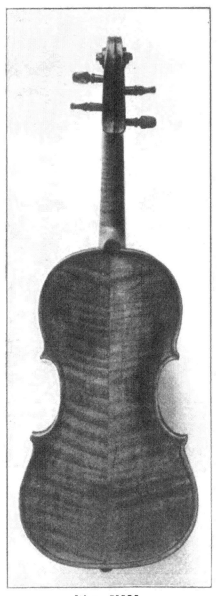

Plate VIII.
VIOLIN, SANTE BALLARINI, ANDREAS GISALBERTI,
c. 1725-34.
Owned by Mr. THOS. NESMITH, U.S.A.

CHAPTER V.

Many Masterpieces Lost, their Identity Removed in Order to substitute other Names for them —Gisalberti's Numerous Types at Different Localities—His Gifted Pupil at Cremona— Birth and Family Connections—Reference to same in Various Books.

OUR knowledge of many of the great luminaries of the liutaro's art in Italy during the sixteenth, seventeenth and eighteenth centuries is almost entirely confined to the bare fact of their having worked in certain places, and left masterpieces behind for our use and admiration.

That some of their supreme efforts and greatest successes have passed out of existence for ever will be acknowledged by all as extremely likely. Many makers of rare ability, not to say genius, have been lost sight of since their cessation from work in the small world wherein they were once probably held in great estimation, but are now quite unknown to a large majority of European connoisseurs.

The great anxiety to obtain fine specimens of well-known masters has been at the root of the matter, and taken advantage of by unscrupulous dealers, who, caring naught for anything but the money consideration, have purposely removed every evidence of identity of one maker, and substituted that which they thought would bring the only desirable end, money.

That this has been the case with Andreas Gisalberti, I have had some amount of evidence pass before me. The

D

striking similarity of his workmanship in many details
with that of his great pupil, Joseph Guarnerius, has been
too much of a temptation where a lucrative return
seemed within reach; the opportunity once caught sight
of has been eagerly seized, and the deception has in
many instances yet to be found out.

Another peculiarity in connection with the work and
manner of its execution by Andreas Gisalberti may be
justly noticed, and that is that notwithstanding the
increase in the number of followers of Antonio Stradivari's style, in different parts of Italy, his manner seems
to have remained undisturbed as that of a man who really
believed in himself. Rough looking and uncouth as some
of his instruments may be called by captious critics, there
is the strong intellectual individuality about them for which
no amount of high finish could compensate, and when in
good preservation and fairly well regulated, the tone is
such as to keep them in the front rank when once they
are recognised.

As is the case with most other makers (perhaps there
is no exception) the violins of Andreas Gisalberti differ
in the degree of power accompanying the fine quality; an
extraordinary amount of both seems to be the essential
in the minds of too many violin players of the present
day. Something that every one will acknowledge to be
exactly as fine as anything yet made, or that has ever
been heard, combined with an overbearing vibratory
power, beside which nothing in the fiddle line can for a
moment live!—that is the combination most eagerly
sought for by so many fiddle and tone fanciers.

When Gisalberti was at Rimini, he added to his previous models two fresh distinct types of violin, the first
being a continuation, or possibly made from the same
blocks and patterns as the Parma instruments, the other
having a stiffer or straighter waist.

They have the same exterior workmanship, but the
interior linings and blocks of the stiff-waisted type are
less massive, although of the same rough or hasty
appearance. This difference would not be easily

accounted for unless we take into consideration the possible assistance found necessary owing to advancing years.

The latest date of Gisalberti's work that has come before me is 1735—he may have worked some time later, I have been told till 1740—it is still under the pseudonym of Sante Ballarini, which, having fastened on to him in former years, he seems to have been known by it.

His gifted pupil, Joseph Guarnerius, was then working at Cremona, sending forth masterpieces that have since been the admiration of the world at large, and possibly, who can tell? the envy of the immediate circle of working liutaros in his adjacent neighbourhood. It is he and his works that will now occupy our attention.

It is to the earliest part of the eighteenth century we will now have our attention directed. A probably unostentatious circumstance, and with nothing about it to cause unusual or gentle surprise, was the fact of a young craftsman leaving the house of his teacher wherein he had for some years been acquiring and storing up the principles and secrets of the art, which he was to practise henceforth for his own personal betterment, and to the pleasure and satisfaction of those by whom he might chance to be patronised—to seek a reputation equal to, if not above, that of the numerous liutaros who were daily making the city of Cremona more and more famous.

A young man, he started off in great confidence that the knowledge he had gained under the guidance of Andreas Gisalberti would prove, if not a veritable mine of wealth, sufficient for all his needs, and likely enough raise his name above those of his family, who had long been established in the city.

His full name has been handed down to us as Giuseppe Antonio Guarneri; to moderns he is known by the Latinised name as seen on his tickets, and which have the second name omitted, and he is thus universally spoken of as Joseph Guarnerius.

That he was born on the 8th of June, 1683, is an established fact, the same having been ascertained from

the registry in the Cathedral in Cremona. On the 11th
he was baptised in the parish church of San Donato.

His father's name was inserted in the registry as
Giovanni Battista Guarneri, and his mother Angela
Locadella. A mere trivial, most ordinary, every day
happening, one would now think, but which may have
been something of an event in the family, which must
have been fairly well and widely known in the fiddle
world of that day. The exact relationship of Giovanni
Battista Guarneri to the others of the well-known family
of the same surname is not yet precisely known. It has
been asserted that tickets have been seen on which
Giuseppe Guarneri stated he was nephew of Andrew,
or, as he would Latinise it, Andrae nepos. These tickets
may, or not, be spurious; I have not seen or met with any
person who had seen them. But allowing these to be
genuine, then G. B. Guarneri, the father of Giuseppe
Guarneri, was brother of Andreas Guarnerius.

Various writers on these particulars of the Guarneri
family have seemingly got either very confused over the
relationship, or have not taken the trouble to scrutinize
all the data at their command.

All that can be gathered concerning them seems to be
agreeable to the assertion made by all writers that the
father of the great Joseph Guarnerius was not a violin
maker, or, at any rate up to the present he has not been
known as one. We, however, may find the announcement made any day that he was, but that he did not
make many instruments, or that his work is not now
known. As instances in connection with this kind of
discovery or resuscitation, may be mentioned the one in
connection with Antonio Mariani, of Pesaro, whose
instruments were said, in the work by Fétis, "to be made
at random, and not even sought after as curiosities"—a
later writer also declaring his disbelief in the existence
of the maker at all. Time, however, settled the question,
and the existence and coming to the market of nearly a
dozen, followed by some work of at least two of the sons,
made the possibility evident, in the assertion of an

enthusiastic collector, that there were at Pesaro about ten of the name working nearly, if not quite, at the same time. Another instance is that of the son of Nicolas Amati, whose name until recently was not to be met with in books or lists of violin makers, yet this maker, who lived a long life, and must have been a fellow patriarch in Cremona with Antonio Stradivari, made many surprisingly beautiful instruments. He is now known as Hieronymus filius Nicolas Amati, and occupies an important position in the estimation of those who have been fortunate in possessing some of his work. The actual relationship of the father, Giovanni Battista Guarneri, with Andrea Guarneri has some little bearing on the subject of the tuition of Giuseppe the Great. Supposing G. B. Guarneri to have been a maker, the most usual or natural course would have been for him to have trained his son in his own atelier, and sent him forth well impressed with his own style, but we have not heard or seen anything of this. On the other hand, if G. B. Guarneri was not a maker, or if we may assume for argument that he was even an actual relative, then possibilities must be admitted that there may not have been much social intercourse between Giovanni Battista and the other Guarneris, but on the contrary, even averseness to it.

Without going to this extreme, the possibility of the comparative strangership between Giuseppe, our subject, and the others of the same name working within hail, is at once seen.

It has so often occurred when a youth has been intended by his parents for some particular calling quite to their liking, that the ruling spirit or latent talent has broken through all restraint, and genius has had its way, with results that historical biography frequently records. If such occurred in the instance of the great Giuseppe Guarneri, there is very little, if any, probability that we shall ever have details.

The fact alone is before us, and in print for the first time, that Giuseppe Antonio Guarneri was apprenticed to, or taught all the necessaries of his craft by, a liutaro who was not a Guarneri, not a Stradivari, nor Amati, but a man independent of all of them, a man of quaint perceptions of beauty in art, but nevertheless having sterling merits in meeting the requirements of the time.

Pausing for a moment, we may take note of the different assertions, ideas and suggestions, concerning the likely pupilage of Joseph Guarnerius that have at different times appeared in print.

One English book, after correctly stating the date and place of Joseph's birth, says he "became a pupil of Stradiuarius, but he was not a mere imitator, and was guided by positive principles." After referring to the absurd fiction about the origin of the "prison Josephs," it states, among other particulars, that "at the commencement of his career, his instruments showed no particular marks of skill." We may suppose these were not evident to the writer, but the public of the time, for whom they were made, must have thought sufficiently well of them to buy them and wish for more ; an encouragement and inducement to continue in the same path which led to the production of so many world-renowned masterpieces.

The well-known work on Antonio Stradivari, by Fétis, says of Joseph Guarnerius that "it even seems that his relationship with the members of his family was not intimate ; for it was neither with Joseph (assumed his cousin), nor yet with Peter Guarnerius that he learnt his art, but with Anthony Stradivarius."

Neither of the above writers gives any details or reference regarding these statements.

It is also further remarked that "Joseph Guarnerius del Jesu worked at Cremona from 1725 to 1745. His first attempts (he was forty-two years of age, reckoning by the dates of his birth and death in the same work) were not marked by any characteristic sign of originality, except a certain indifference in the choice of his materials, in the forms, which are variable, and in the varnish."

Really, the author points out in the latter part of this paragraph, the only essentials in which originality could be expressed ; if these were the exceptions, of what did the peculiarity in the main consist, wherein Joseph did not manifest any " characteristic sign of originality ? "

Most of the books in which Joseph Guarnerius's career is touched upon, repeat one after another the same kind of thoughtless assertions, taken perhaps from the same original sources, putting them forward as accepted facts in connection with tradition. Forty-two years of age is a rather advanced stage in the lifetime of ordinary men at which to commence an entirely novel career, and it is very remarkable, if not quite unknown, for one during the last twenty years of his life to become an acknow-ledged master of a difficult art, and, at the end, leave behind him a growing and imperishable fame.

No writer that I am aware of has pecked at this seeming great inconsistency, and it may not have occurred to any one to search into the matter with the object of finding out how, or in what direction, Joseph Guarnerius was engaged during his early manhood, up to the very late time in life at which he has been credited with having first constructed his violins.

An answer might be hazarded by those who would be anxious to have their creed still upheld, that there was a possibility of his having worked as an assistant to one of the important makers of Cremona, and that circumstances unknown and only indirectly connected with business, may have been in the way; or, as being somewhat in harmony with this, the instance might be cited of old Andreas Amati while in Brescia assisting a much younger man who had brought out a new form of musical instru-ment—to wit, the violin.

This would be reasonable so far as it went, but on the other hand, there is an unanswerable rejoinder that would naturally come to mind in the discussion, that the pupil or even assistant of long standing always reproduces, more or less, in his manner of work, the prominent features of style belonging to his master, and the instance of old Andreas Amati would actually go very strongly to help this, his work showing distinctly his natural tendency to refinement and delicacy, while acting upon suggestions thrown out by his master's more rugged style of workmanship.

Taking up the argument of the possibility of Joseph's working under the flag of some maker of importance in Cremona till the time of his supposed *début* as a master liutaro, we look round and about in vain for a possible or likely practitioner with and from whom he could have been helping and receiving instruction. His own style at the time—1725, and through the succeeding years—is so highly artistic, and the individuality so forcible, that any effort to fix upon any known maker of the same locality as at all likely to be his master shortly before that becomes futile. He was, in fact, at this period himself a leading light, influencing other makers near and far, who in turn reflected his grand qualities in their own works to the enhancement of their known reputation. The old hypothesis and statements so often referred to and repeated by writers, that Joseph Guarnerius was a pupil of Antonio Stradivari must thus necessarily crumble to pieces ; no two makers could, in the manifestations of their artistic tendencies, ideas of proportion, and direction of line, be more opposed. Those who have even gone so far as to write of the resemblance of some of Joseph's violins to those of Antonio's, had better be left alone ; there would be no profit attached to a contest concerning assertions in this direction, and in which there is so much oblique mental vision, if not total absence of artistic perception.

A more reasonable view of the subject was taken by another writer, who, in the absence of any data of a reliable kind, went fairly to work upon the probabilities indicated by general appearance and workmanship.

The conclusions arrived at were that the most likely teacher was his cousin, known to connoisseurs of the present day as Joseph filius Andrea, who, the writer stated, " is the only maker in whose productions we can find the strong similarity needed." To help this, the fact is referred to that Joseph filius was the " senior by many years."

There is much indication of sound reasoning in this,
but the deductions for general apparent indication leading
to the hypothetical teacher were much spoilt, if not
totally upset, by the introduction of the name of Gasparo
da Salo, to whom, the writer says, Joseph "seems to have
turned as the maker whose lead he wished to follow."
Referring to the detail of the soundhole of Gaspar's, the
writer says that "Guarneri del Gesu retained its pointed
form.   Next comes the outline of the body, where, again,
there is much affinity to the type of Gasparo da Salo."

Of this last, criticism is scarcely necessary, as the
particular specimens in the mind's eye at the time
possibly suggested it.   But the retention of the " pointed
form " of the Gasparo soundhole is quite another matter ;
the writer was doubtless mixing up the two old Brescian
masters, Gasparo da Salo and Giovanni Paolo Maggini
as inconsistently as later commentators have Stradivari
and Guarneri.

As these two masters last mentioned were different in
their conceptions of their ideal soundhole, so were the
two first.   Gasparo da Salo's soundholes were, all of
them, distinctly opposed in intention and execution to the
" Gothic " or pointed style introduced later by his
famous pupil and successor, Maggini.   The dealers have
for long mixed up these masters, occasionally flavouring
the composition by the addition of a quaint Mariani
father or son as occasion prompted.

Another writer, seemingly dubious as to the propriety
of being led along servilely on the lines adopted by
preceding authors, states that "it was a long-accepted
conclusion that Joseph del Gesu was a pupil of the still
greater Antonio Stradivari, but a more intimate acquaintance with his early violins has somewhat unsettled that
opinion.   Like those belonging to a similar period of
Stradivari himself, Joseph's early works, displaying few
marks of what is called originality, are, more or less,
reproductions of the form and style handed down by
Nicolas Amati to ancestors of the Guarneri family."   As
the most famous of this family, Nicolas, was living close

up to the end of the seventeenth century, and with great
probability working when "Joseph del Gesu" was from
five to seven years of age, the public may reasonably
expect that something will yet turn up respecting these
particular "ancestors"; at present a veil obscures them
and their work.

The writer in mentioning "Joseph's early works,"
doubtless was referring to those made in 1725 or 1730, as
he remarks besides that "the earliest known tickets date
from 1725;" here again is some indication of the
"accepted conclusion" that Joseph was a pupil of
Stradivari up to about that time, the dates being given by
earlier writers as those connected with his early efforts,
these be it remembered, being made when he must have
been at the age of forty-two.

It is this remarkable improbability, coupled with its
gross inconsistency, that must appeal to every one not
having already a rooted prejudice against the upsetting
of old settled ideas and supposed facts.

The world in general easily settles down in treating a
bold assertion, however unreasonable or preposterous it
may appear to a few, as solid and even established truth,
if it is not soon attacked or strangled early in its career.

Thus with the present part of our subject under consideration, no one—no writer at least—seems to have
referred to any authority or data for the hitherto supposed
fact of the teacher of Joseph Guarnerius being Antonius
Stradivarius. Not one, even if feeling able, has probed
the matter, argued it out, or at any time tested the stability
of its own merits from their foundation on any facts.

Some early writer may only have had a passing
thought in his mind that Joseph's tuition was possibly, if
not probably, under the great Cremonese, thinking him
the only master capable of training a man of such very
strong individuality and genius as Joseph Guarnerius.

The thought, hastily conceived, found its way into print.
Remaining unquestioned and uncontradicted, it assumed
gradually, by repetition and quotation, the superficial
appearance of a positive fact.

Thus we find "the long-accepted conclusion" firmly implanted in the mind of the reading but unanalyzing portion of the public, who are unwilling to have any long fixed ideas much disturbed, not to say entirely eradicated.

Like many long-rooted weeds on untrimmed land where much time and trouble has often to be expended before the desirable condition is arrived at, in the present instance there will doubtless be many people still clinging with great tenacity to their old beliefs, notwithstanding the cessation of the necessity being put before them plain as the blue sky above.

When the young Giuseppe Antonio Guarneri, or, as he is better known to us, Joseph Guarnerius, left his teacher Andrea Gisalberti, there was in front of him such an array of talent, among whom forthwith he was to work his way, that if not sufficiently imbued with that self-consciousness, reliance, and determination which we find is so plainly indicated on his world-renowned master-pieces, he might, with good cause, have shrunk from entering the arena, except as a low-rate contendant, or insignificant, if even a useful help to one.

That there were many good artificers of the last class in Cremona, we may put it down as fairly certain; men who could always work well under guidance, but who would recoil from any undertaking where there was responsibility.

CHAPTER VI.

JOSEPH GUARNERIUS'S FIRST APPEARANCE—EARLY
WORK AND TICKETS—HIS CONTEMPORARIES—THE
CONDITION OF THE ART IN CREMONA AT THE TIME
—THE PRECISE POSITION OF HIS FIRST ATELIER
NOT KNOWN—JOSEPH'S FIRST TICKETS IN HIS
VIOLINS—FULFILLING THE REQUIREMENT OF THE
HOUR—MODIFICATIONS IN HIS DESIGNS—HIS
WOOD AND VARNISH—HIS MODE OF AFFIXING
THE NECK.

IN the absence of any reliable data concerning
Joseph's first appearance before the public, we may
assume, with some degree of confidence, that it
occurred about the time, or immediately after, the days
of his tuition or apprenticeship were accomplished. This
would be about the year 1704, when he would be twenty-
one years old. He may have remained working still
under his master's guidance as an improver for another
year, and it was then, if not before, that he started as
master liutaro.

For a moment let us glance at the general condition of
the little world of Italian liutaros in the city of Cremona
at the time when Joseph Guarnerius thought it ripe for
going forth on his own responsibility, and battling with
the world.

There was, high and above all others, and in all probability receiving his due share of honour from his fellow
craftsmen, Antonio Stradivari, then acknowledged chief
in matters pertaining to the art of the liutaro, his two

sons working with him, Hieronymus, son of Nicolas Amati, and several of the Ruggieris.

Among the probable workers there at the time, before going to the other cities with which their names are more immediately identified, were Lorenzo Guadagnini, Carlo Giuseppe Testore, besides an interesting little tribe of makers of lesser fame, and others whose work alone remains to us, and who may have been well known even if without great renown.

The whole of these working simultaneously, and apparently with fair patronage, must have looked a somewhat formidable array, with whom he would have to compete. Besides the reputation of the well-known and established makers at Cremona being in his way, a seeming obstacle to progress, other considerations had to be studied—those connected with the character of the work itself that he was to put forth. The liutaro's art had about reached its climax in the estimation of the *dilettanti ;* there was no room for extra finish, beautiful proportion, or elegance of line ; the Amatis and the living Stradivari were doing, and had done, all that seemed possible in those directions. What, then, was there to take up and improve upon ?

There must have seemed but one answer to this—none ! Henceforth a new maker must be content with a position at the best scarcely reaching that occupied by the recognised masters.

To these considerations, Joseph Guarnerius very likely inclined but little, if attending to them at all. There was one direction open, suggested by the advance of musical composition and the efforts of the virtuosi of the day.

If not actually appearing to him as a want that he would endeavour to meet with the means at his command, there was the opportunity.

His master, Andreas Gisalberti—at this time the nickname of Sante Ballarini had not yet been associated with him and his work—had produced instruments having among them special qualities of tone that must have appeared to many musicians as surprising in its body, sweetness, and penetrating power.

This was a direction that could be worked in ; indications were present that good patronage would eventually follow perseverance in it.

This kind or quality of tone became his purpose to produce, develop, and continue with a fixed determination which he followed to the last.

Separating himself from Gisalberti at an appropriate time suitable to his views, he started business forthwith.

Settled down in his own working apartments, we can imagine his anticipating good support from those who were to become acquainted with the quality of tone with which his name was hereafter to become associated.

Fresh patrons would be desirable, and these must know his name as distinct from other makers of the same surname.

His ticket had, therefore, to be composed, and placed, as was the custom with other makers, in his violins. The usual way was adopted—that of having the name and century date surrounded by a border engraved on a block, from which a number could be printed, the precise year being added by pen and ink.

The accompanying facsimile is perhaps the earliest ticket used by Joseph Guarnerius.

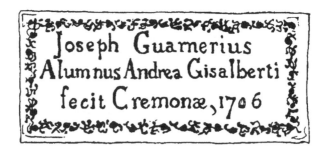

On this ticket is the assertion plainly enough that

Joseph Guarnerius was the pupil of Andreas Gisalberti. The nickname, Sante Ballarini, does not appear to have been used at this time, but after the year 1717 at Rimini. That tickets of Andreas Gisalberti were issued at Cremona for some time before his removal to Parma is at once pointedly evident.

As the Gisalberti ticket, previously reproduced, is dated 1716, just ten years after the Joseph Guarnerius one of 1706, Gisalberti may have removed to Parma about the same year or a little earlier, when Joseph Guarnerius would be thrown upon his own resources, seeking for patronage we may suppose among the comparatively small world of patrons of the liutaro's art, and the reference to his teacher would naturally enough seem to him almost if not quite necessary.

In this one respect the times and circumstances then obtaining in Cremona would differ but little from those of the present day. Thus, when an assistant has been identified for a length of time with an establishment of renown or widely known, and starts a business of his own, a very frequent, if not invariable practice, is for the young man to announce his former connection with the better known establishment. This, in the pianoforte trade, is of constant occurrence, as all readers will at once recognise.

During the times of which we are treating, when cities and towns of even premier importance were without their numerous newspapers of different political creeds receiving instant news from all parts of the earth, it is quite clear that people in business could not as at the present time have addressed themselves to the world at large by means of open advertisement in a newspaper; their announcement of what they had to dispose of was mainly on their own premises, and except by the sign outside, they were known almost solely among the limited circles requiring the particular commodity.

The business of the liutaro in the Italian cities and towns must have seemed of quite a retiring or modest kind.

As with many occupations carried on in continental cities at the present day, there would often be nothing evident to the stranger in the street of a brisk business being carried on at the upper part. If conducted on a more substantial scale, the lower would bear but little indication of what was going on in other portions of the premises, one or two articles perhaps being perceptible only on a closer approach, these being purposely kept out of the direct rays of the sun and for coolness.

We may never get at the knowledge of the exact spot where young Joseph Guarnerius first opened up or commenced his business as an independent liutaro.

It seems scarcely probable that at the outset he worked on the premises in the Piazzi di San Domenico, a position that might have required more means than were at first at the command of the young artist. We might look to any other part of Cremona as being a likely neighbourhood in which his early works were completed.

The neighbourhood or the sphere of influence exercised by the makers well known, firmly established, or eminent in their craft, would not be the most tempting position for opening up a business connection unless one appeared at hand established and ready for taking over at once.

A conjecture might not be unreasonably hazarded that, as the precise period of Andreas Gisalberti's departure from Cremona to Parma is unascertained, Joseph Guarnerius may have taken over, under his own management, the premises where he had been trained and for years been working.

Doubtless the circle of supporting patrons with which Gisalberti was connected, would hope to have, if possible, after his departure, the same class and style of work as they had been in the habit of receiving at his hands.

For this the young apprentice with fully served time would not think of making much difference, if any, in the general appearance of his work in comparison with that of his recent master; he may, in common with most pupils, have esteemed the style of his master as superior to any other that had been scrutinised by him.

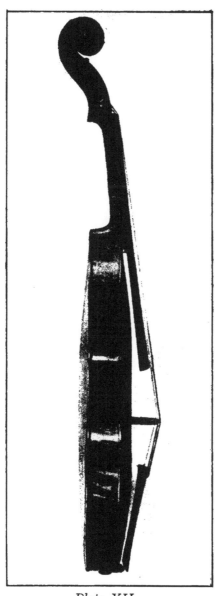

Plate XII.
VIOLIN, JOSEPH GUARNERIUS, WITH TICKET, 1706.
Owned by Mr. H. PETHERICK.

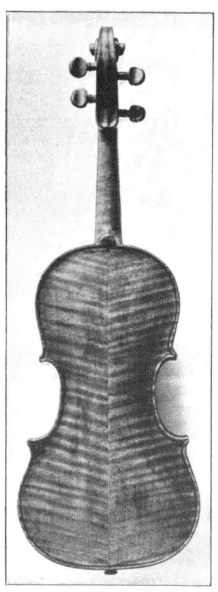

Plate XI.
VIOLIN, JOSEPH GUARNERIUS, WITH TICKET, 1706.
Owned by Mr. H. PETHERICK.

Taking this view, we may claim as collateral critics those who have so strenuously maintained the necessary connection of style or mannerism of the pupil and master. It might be added that in the majority of instances, the tinge of the master is indelible.

In the greater number of the well known Italian liutaros this is very plainly evident.

Maggini's early work is so like that of his teacher, Gasparo da Salo, that many connoisseurs might call it identical until the smaller differences of detail are perceived. It is so like, that dealers have often disposed of the work of one as being that of the other. Andreas Guarnerius is another whose early style is so akin to that of his master, Nicolas Amati, that the instruments of the former have been and continue to be sold over and over again as those of the latter. Francesco Ruggieri has been similarly treated; the Gaglianos in like manner followed one another in rotation, until too depraved in their art to make anything respectable; and of Grancino and Testore the same may be said. Early works of Antonio Stradivari have been also, until their authenticity has been recognised later, many times sold in times gone by as being veritable if not very characteristic specimens of his master.

With regard to the two masters, the subject of our consideration, the position has been reversed. The reason is sufficiently clear; the immense subsequent reputation of the pupil, while the name of the master was gradually, from some cause, subsiding into obscurity, has been a strong temptation to unscrupulous or nonproficient traders to pass off the "something like" for the "real thing."

To return now to the young liutaro whom we may suppose as working strictly on the lines laid down or followed by his master.

The requirements of the class of patrons who doubtless had long been accustomed to look upon Gisalberti's productions as being the most excellent supply to their wants, must be satisfied and up to, if possible, the same degree of particular quality.

E

That this was in the power of young Joseph Guarnerius, all connoisseurs will readily admit; his training, his apparent means of obtaining the exact quality and growth of pine for the upper tables or soundboards of his violins, all being evidenced by his work taken as a whole.

But there is one consideration that must not be overlooked in our criticism. There was the requirement of the hour; the fulfilment was in the hands of the man found ready and determined to do his best.

Had the man been only of a stamp such as can be seen upon many works of an even respectable standing in the same branch of art, Joseph Guarnerius might have been known to but few connoisseurs of the present day, and only by them as a quaint, unrecognised Italian liutaro.

He was not of such a disposition, but being a man of the most marked individuality, so noticeable during the middle and later portion of his career, it could not be expected in reason that evidence of it would be absent in his earliest works, notwithstanding the very close alliance with the ideas of his teacher.

We are fortunately able to make a fair comparison between the work of Joseph Guarnerius of 1706 and that of Andreas Gisalberti, as exhibited in the several specimens which have been reproduced for these pages. Supposing the separation of master and pupil to have occurred within a year, or very shortly before the construction of this violin, 1706, we can perceive already a hint thrown out as to the direction in which a possible development of his powers might manifest itself. This is in the lengthening or spreading of the curves, in parts where his master's lines may have seemed to him somewhat cramped.

This, doubtless, was with the view of introducing more of the gracefulness combined with breadth of style in design, and which was to be a retained peculiarity as he advanced in his studies. It is further particularly noticeable in the form and position of the soundholes : these, while having strongly over them the Gisalberti characteristics, are lengthened and placed more upright, the backward reach of the upper part being also got rid of. There is still the determined curl of the lower part with the fully-developed and rather broad lower wing, so constant with his master.

The waist curves—or C's as some people know them, and which generally form the principal means by which the stamp of individuality or impression of peculiarity of type is imparted to the design—have a larger reach, although not so deeply cut inward when near the centre. This at once modifies the general aspect—as regards mere form—at a glance; there is less of a tendency to uncouthness and a marked advance towards grace.

Other details in the work show much less change—the purfling in material and mode of insertion is the same, but the border is less broad and obtrusive, while there is some attempt at delicacy. It is not very bold or much raised, nor beyond the average of the moderately elevated types of Cremonese violins. There is also much evidence of his habit of working, the rather hasty go-ahead way, noticeable in even his most finished specimens.

With regard to the materials used, we might assume that these were almost compulsory, as a sudden departure or selection of a different class of wood for either upper or lower table would have imparted a different character, and been prejudicial to the sale among the class of people who had respected, as a maker, Andreas Gisalberti.

Accordingly we find the wood, as regards appearance, identical with that used by Joseph's master. There is the same broad curled sycamore of the best quality, having the well marked or nutmeggy appearance peculiar to almost all the finest productions of the eminent liutaros of Italy.

The back is in two pieces, with the curls rising a little from the centre upwards; this is the manner that Joseph favoured mostly at all times; those with the downward direction are comparatively few in number. It is fairly regular, but free from the mechanical stiffness and

E2

monotonous repetition seen in the productions of many
makers of an inferior order of merit.

The pine at once suggests to the eye of the critic a
selected quality, no first-to-hand stuff or obligatory use
of material of sonorous quality regardless of mere
appearance. With many makers this latter has without
doubt been the necessity of the moment.

The threads are fine, although firm, and may be
termed moderately open, but not of constant regular
width apart. They are fairly straight, but not rigidly so.
The general aspect of the pine used throughout the
career of Joseph Guarnerius suggests that it has been
drawn from the same district as that used by his
master.

The peculiar character of the wood noticeable as
having been used by Joseph for individual specimens, we
shall have to consider later on. For the present it will
perhaps be sufficient, while passing, to observe that
although the general character, or variety of pine used
by master and pupil seems to point to its being identical,
or having been probably obtained from the same forest,
where it grew under like conditions of soil and climate,
there is more variety of grain in the pine from which
Andrea Gisalberti made his upper tables or sound boards,
than that favoured by Joseph Guarnerius.

For this, considering our very limited knowledge of
fact in connection with the subject, it is not possible
to assign a reason. Gisalberti may have been less
particular as to general effective appearance, so long as
the essentials were present for imparting the desired
quantity of tone.

Although there is this variableness in the grain of the
pine, more especially as regards the width apart of the
threads, yet up to the present very little of the close,
even, almost mathematical regularity of the threads seen
with so many instruments of the earlier Cremonese and
Venetian schools, has been met with. The particular soil
or meteorological phenomena of the district may have
had some influence over this.

That the mere width of grain, or its straightness, has little or nothing to do with the quality or quantity of tone emitted by the instrument, there is .abundant evidence.

As an example we may take, almost haphazard, the violins by Giovanni Paolo Maggini. The first one taken might be possibly one with a front table of wide grained pine, the impression received at once being that this maker selected a very open grained timber, in order, as some theorists would have it, to get that "great breadth and voluminous tone" for which he has been so renowned. Another one turns up, when lo and behold! the threads of the pine are so close together as to give much trouble in individualising or counting them ; the critics are dumbfounded, looking upon the whole affair as an unfathomable mystery.

The same instrument coming under the eyes of another set of critics, is declared to be almost conclusive evidence in support of their hypothesis that the good old makers, and Maggini in particular, used wood cut from towering venerable giants of the forest, that had for ages, as poetically but erroneously described by Longfellow, "in Tyrolean forest vast, rocked and wrestled with the blast." The "Tyrolean forest" did not supply the wood for the Italian liutaros, but for those of the Stainer and Klotz school ; the material is recognised easily.

Good for the imagination this last, but not the digestion of hard facts. The knotted old denizen of the forest for hundreds of years is scarcely the tree that we should expect, when under an altered condition of facture it is to be made subservient to man's requirements, to throw out or impart a dulcet and sympathetic quality of sound to strings held in bondage and completely under its con-trol. Should we not rather expect some favoured valley or mountain side, sheltered from the cold blast, and specially favourable for the growth of a rapidly maturing tree, with but few branches or knots, and these of small size sparsely appearing.

Such a result is what seems apparent in most of the

wood used for the violins sent forth by the celebrated
Italian liutaros.

Some critics will, perhaps, be inclined to dispute this,
and refer to what has seemed to them to be coarse
threaded pine used by Maggini and other earlier makers.
The rejoinder to this is that the coarse, hard looking
thread, or bate, is only apparent and not real. When
under repair, it has sometimes been found necessary to
make an even surface at a part of the interior for affixing
some fresh wood. In doing so these threads are found
not to be really hard in the ordinary sense of the term,
like modern coarse pine, the growth appearing to have
been rapid, and very little of the hard resinous quality
present.

With regard to the varnish used by Joseph Guarnerius
for his early work, the specimen of 1706 referred to
affords some indication. It does not appear to have
been an invariable rule with the pupils of the eminent
liutaros of the old Italian schools to have used, or even
been initiated into, the mysteries of the art of varnishing.

With the earlier masters it was much more general
for the pupil to continue the same type of varnish as his
master. In some instances, although having the same
qualities in common, there is considerable difference,
owing, it may be, to some variation in the manipulation,
if not in the exact proportion of the ingredients of the
composition.

Thus we find all the known pupils of the Amatis
following in their masters' steps, those also of Gasparo
da Salo and Maggini, besides others among the liutaros
of Venice.

Not to be lost sight of is the fact of many masters in
their early days using a light coloured varnish, and as
years rolled by, giving more and more preference for
varnishes of a deeper or more decided brown hue.

The Amatis seem to have been content for years with
their amber or orange colour, now and then making a
departure for a bright copper or deep orange, with an
occasional specimen of rich transparent brown.

With regard to Andrea Gisalberti, he being to us moderns an almost unknown maker, or one whose past reputation has yet to be resuscitated and brought more completely to light, enough specimens of his life's work are not to hand whereby we could classify or divide them into periods. Like all other busy men, there is the greatest probability that there was some distinctive mannerism peculiar to his early working career as distinguishable from his later period.

Already there seems to be enough evidence to suggest that his fancy, in common with so many, if not a very large majority of makers, was for a lighter or less densely constituted varnish than that used by him in his later days.

In this respect he was followed by his renowned pupil. The specimen referred to, made in 1706, has a lighter coloured varnish than those of his master with which I have become acquainted. It is transparent, free from the glassy hardness of a large majority of the yellow varnishes of the Milanese and Neapolitan schools, not to mention the occasional ones of almost all the others. As a rule these yellow, and to the eye, most inelastic of varnishes, when examined in a strong light, or with a magnifying glass, prove to be covered with minute fractures, more or less sharp according to the degree of flintiness.

The varnish of this specimen of Joseph Guarnerius's early work is free from this, and partakes more of the consistency of the soft yellows of the Pesaro makers and some of the other members of the Brescian school. It is clear, although at a short distance it does not strike the eye at once as being very brilliant. The threads of the pine are very distinctly seen, and the curls of the sycamore flash well underneath when the violin is moved about in the light.

It does not, however, give the impression of having been made or laid on like that of his master; if it is as clear, it is less limpid, and there is not that appearance of liquidity almost suggestive of its still being soft and almost wet as if done yesterday. This is somewhat suggestive that the pupil may have—in the varnish as well as the outline—thus early manifested that spirit of independence and individuality which was to develop and become so marked a characteristic in his after career.

A few words may be said regarding the interior of the violin.

At this time the manner of attaching the linings running round from the corner to the end blocks is the same as that of his master, and they are likewise of pine. They are not let into the middle blocks. The upper block having been renewed, nothing can be said about the original except that in all probability it had the one nail driven through to the root of the neck, as usual with Gisalberti, and which his pupil continued as a regular rule to the last.

This, it may be observed, was in accordance with the practice at the time of affixing the neck before closing up or glueing on the upper table. The upper rib was made from one piece, and continuous—that is, when length of material was at hand—passed round the mould, the ends reaching to the corner blocks, bent to make them fit, and then fixed. The part passing over the end block was, as a matter of course, glued to it. There was thus an even surface along over the course of the upper ribs round from corner to corner. The neck was then fitted on to the centre, not always mathematically true; it may be presumed that a hole was perforated in the block about the centre, and a nail of about an inch and a half in length on the average driven through into the root of the neck, until the flat head of the nail was flush with the curved inner surface of the block.

This nail, when an instrument has survived the ravages of time, wear and tear and accidents, reaching us in what is known as its original condition, is looked upon by repairers as an abomination, giving much trouble, and worrying both his tools and his temper.

Now-a-days when once out no nail ever enters again; that is, if the repairer is at all up to date in his methods of working. The hole wherein the nail was lately located is either filled up with a plug of wood, or left open for the future antiquarian to marvel at. The instrument is closed up and the graft or new neck let in according to the skill and care exercised, with air-tight exactness, in the manner to be seen in any ordinary modern violin.

From the universal practice among the old Italian violin makers of inserting this nail, or sometimes three, in addition to the glueing for holding fast the neck to the body of the violin, it would appear that their confidence in glue was limited, although that which they used was light in colour and of first-rate quality.

Among the several probable reasons for this there was, firstly, the changing from the old Brescian custom of making neck and upper block in one piece. This was no doubt for convenience in placing all the blocks on the mould during one stage, at the same time facilitating the handling of the structure before finally closing up.

The neck and block, however, when made separately, had to be fitted carefully, or they would be liable to part under the influence of damp or rough usage, it being absolutely necessary that the neck should be held securely; the nail was therefore driven through the block into it (from the inside, of course), before the body was closed up.

The result was just a little too much cohesiveness, that is, from the modern repairer's point of view, as he is oftentimes justly desirous of keeping as many original parts perfect as possible, while it is necessary to lengthen the neck or put a new graft without injuring the block, or perhaps removing the upper table, and the trouble is then very great.

In some parts of Italy it was the custom to insert two nails, and at times three; the trouble was, therefore, increased in these instances.

Both Andreas Gisalberti and his pupil, Joseph Guarnerius, appear to have kept invariably to the habit of fixing the neck on the body of the violin by one nail.

The continuous rib was not cut through in the least ; the flat surface of the root of the neck was simply placed against it in a freshly-glued state, and the nail driven in.

Although not a regular habit, there was occasionally one thing in common with both artists concerning the thicknesses left in the upper table : this was in leaving the part round about and below the sound-holes a little thicker than any other part.

CHAPTER VII.

Of Thicknesses—The Sizes of the Violins by Joseph and his Teacher—The Tuition of Gisalberti, who is said to have married into the Mariani Family — Many of his Works probably still Extant but Undiscovered.

MUCH has been written about the thicknesses of the upper and lower tables in the violins of the great makers. And in this purely mechanical department of the art of the liutaro, many have declared that in a certain system, as they called it, lay the secret of the splendid tone of Joseph, and that other masters obtained their tone by a different system. The idea seems to have had its incubation in the brain of the connoisseurs owing to the fact of the discovery in one or two specimens of the position of the thicknesses referred to. These critics, however, do not seem to have been aware of the same system —if such it can appropriately be called—having been not unfrequently worked upon by makers of other schools and classes of tone-quality, among whom may be mentioned some of the Testores of Milan, besides others of the Stradivari school.

All persons who have directed their attention to the construction of violins, old and new, must be well aware of the numberless attempts that have been made to get a particular quality of tone by means of different graduations of thickness of different parts of the instrument. Had there been anything in this beyond what may be concerned in the proper emission of the quality and inherent with the tree from which the wood was obtained, the difficulties would long ago have been surmounted, being a mere mechanical arrangement; Stradivaris, Amatis, Guarneris, and other articles of rarity and price, would have been equalled or even excelled by the aid of the modern tools and appliances at hand.

The masters of tone production have, however, declared as emphatically as they could through their works, that their secret—if it was such in the ordinary sense of the term—was not to be unravelled by the mechanician.

To resume our comparisons between master and pupil. There is in the measurement of their violins a general agreement, somewhat distinct and peculiar. It is a fact generally known that an ordinary full-sized specimen of Stradivari's work will measure very closely, if not exactly, fourteen English inches in length from end to end, leaving out the button. This appears to have been his regular full size. Less numerous patterns are met with an eighth of an inch shorter, while others are over the fourteen and up to a quarter of an inch longer; these latter are very exceptional.

With Joseph Guarnerius and his teacher this is reversed—their general length appears, up to the beginning of his late period, to be an eight or sixteenth under fourteen inches. That this was in conformity with some set rule or requirement from a business point of view, and from which it was undesirable to depart, seems certain; no theory of artistic proportion, or of size in connection with voluminousness or tonal properties of the materials used, seems to account for it. The requirements of a particular class of patrons were probably among the most solid reasons, although we are here again met with the absence of full information concerning many social peculiarities of the period, and which might bear upon the subject.

Comparing the two makers—master and pupil—with respect to style generally, and in detail, we may again touch upon the Stradivari teaching theory.

A long time back it was pointed out that any resemblance between the work at any time of Stradivari and Joseph Guarnerius is so remote as to be unworthy of consideration. That this is really the case has of late years been more and more evident, until it may now be said that the tracing of Stradivari's teaching through the resemblance of the work of the two makers has been given up as leading to no certain result. That the method of procedure was the most likely to bear good fruit there is no doubt, as reference to other makers and their pupils have in other instances so strongly. helped it.

In the case of Gisalberti and Guarneri, however, the teacher, in most violent contrast to his pupil, has suffered almost total obliteration from the list of known makers, small or great, and has been held in remembrance by only very few of his compatriots.

Turning aside again for a moment, but in connection with the above remarks on analogy in work, my hypothesis may be referred to as to the inspiration, if not actual tuition, of Andreas Gisalberti, from some member of the Mariani family of Pesaro. In connection with this I received information from a connoisseur that while travelling in Italy, he had heard of a tradition that Gisalberti, otherwise Santa Ballarini, was known at Ancona (about thirty-five miles from Pesaro) as a man of universal talent, a natural musician, a writer of sacred music, and on intimate terms with a clerical dignity of the church there; that he was a sculptor as well, and that he carved many wall brackets, besides doing other artistic work.

A not less interesting item of information was that "he was said to have married into the Mariani family" —the violin makers of that name. This, if true, gives a strong confirmation of the aptness of my conjecture.

I may mention, with regard to this last, that my informant had not read any remarks as to the probable inspiration of Gisalberti's work, nor heard of my hypothesis.

Some time back there turned up a violin with a ticket worded as follows :—

ANDREA GISALBERTI

CREMONENSIS

FECIT BOZZOLO 1717

It was not his invariable custom to date his tickets.

Bozzolo is situated some sixteen or seventeen miles east of Cremona, and this may have been his first resting stage during his wanderings after leaving his future famous pupil.

It is quite within probability that more, if not many, of Gisalberti's works will come to light now that a hunt for them has commenced. During his Cremona period —of which it is to be hoped some violins will hereafter appear—and while he was at Parma, where his stay was sufficiently long to warrant the use of printed tickets, he must have made many instruments which were afterwards dispersed about the country, some of them possibly still surviving the ravages of time and the repairers.

To return again to Joseph Guarnerius. We left him a young man of twenty-three years of age, issuing violins with his own ticket with the announcement that he was the pupil of Andreas Gisalberti. It is a matter of much regret that of the next few years no specimen of his work is at hand for reference. There is an unexplained gap which may yet be found to be not for ever bare of specimens, and those which are destined to come to light will be interesting in the extreme.

It has been said in Italy, that Joseph Guarnerius, like his teacher, wandered for some time from place to place, and if this should prove to be true, it would account for the blank after the year 1706. Be this as it may, we can only deal at present with what facts are within our reach, and therefore passing over from 1706 to 1714, we have under our consideration another specimen from the hand of Joseph Guarnerius, whose ticket of the time is thus :—

Joseph Guarnerius
Alumnus Andreæ Gisalberti
fecit in Cremonæ 1714

It would be very interesting to know whether this instrument was one of a number made by him at the time, or only a few interspersed among others of different or the earlier characteristics. Years back I met with another of the same type, but which had been robbed of its ticket. At the time, to me it was an interesting, well preserved old Italian violin, but being unable to definitely decide as to its authorship, I had to be content with noting down as many of its peculiarities as possible under the circumstances.

As I have not been able to keep in touch with it, the owner having since that time died, the violin may now be in some collector or player's hands unrecognised, except so far as its strong Italian character and fine tonal qualities might be perceptible to the eye and ear of the owner.

The difference in many points of detail between this specimen of Joseph's work and the earlier one illustrated in these pages, is so great, that at first sight the connection in general style, outline and modelling, is difficult to grasp; nevertheless, after a while, the individuality of many parts is perceptibly the same in both.

Another interesting specimen of this period is Mr. Robson's violin (*See Plates XIII., XIV., and XV.*).

The cause of apparent divergence is, in the first place, the enormous advance in boldness, both in conception of the design and its execution. There is here the first indication of the peculiar power of Joseph Guarnerius, in giving an impression of largeness, apparently without effort, even suggesting a want of consciousness of the

acquirement of the quality possessed by so few in all the
domain of art.

There is present an evident intention to break the
bonds that may have held him for some years in close
tie with the mannerism of his teacher, with the result
that at one bound, he had found himself free. He had
found for himself a fresh line of ideas in design from
which there would probably be no turning back.

But notwithstanding this, some peculiarities, seemingly
almost innate with him, but which had really been
instilled into his system during his early practice under
Andrea Gisalberti, could not be suppressed, and still
clung to him.

These were little touches dispersed over the whole
instrument requiring all the independence and fecundity
of resource at the command of Joseph to entirely get
rid of, supposing him anxious to do so.

There is, even in the work of his latter days, when
most free from this influence, good ground for suspicion
of a still lurking admiration for some of his master's
idiosyncrasies ; we shall again have occasion to refer to
this, when his late work is under consideration.

With the first glance at the instrument, the parts to
which the attention is drawn principally are the massive
border, and the extremely bold purfling, thick enough to
have adorned a good sized viola.

The general contour is much changed from the 1706
specimen, there is the flatter curving at the waist, this
appearing to be much longer, from its gentle progress
from point to point, and seeming more complex than it
really is.

There is an emphasis or inward cutting of the
line at the upper part, which suggests an idea that
the designer projected a further originality of form with
a little more squareness at the under part of the
shoulder.

Treating this as a slight experimental curve, he
probably abstained from often repeating it, from an
apparently natural dislike to anything approaching

Plate XIII.
VIOLIN, JOSEPH GUARNERIUS, C. 1710-13.
Owned by Mr. P. A. ROBSON.

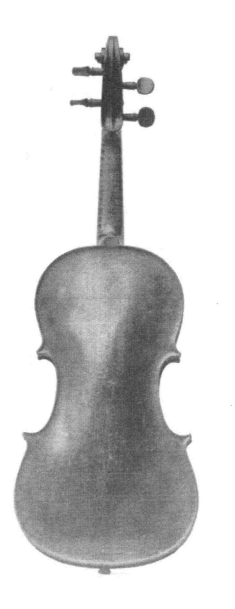

Plate XIV.
VIOLIN, JOSEPH GUARNERIUS, C. 1710-13.
Owned by Mr. P. A. ROBSON.

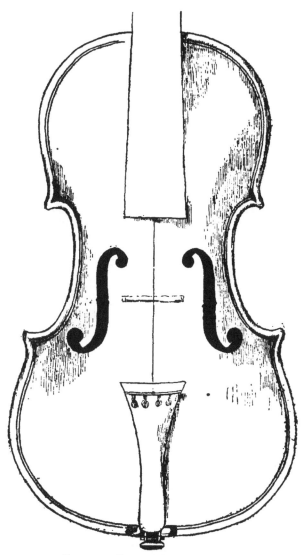

JOSEPH GUARNERIUS, 1714.

F

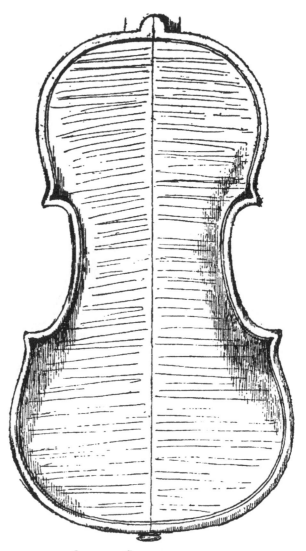

JOSEPH GUARNERIUS, 1714.

abruptness in this part, and which defect he seems to have carefully avoided all through his career.

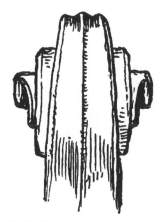

BACK VIEW OF SCROLL, JOSEPH
GUARNERIUS, 1714.

The purfling with the wide centre of light coloured wood, possibly sycamore, is enclosed between thinner lines of black wood, which, from its dark colour and sharpness of cutting, may be ebony; the difficulty in bending this unwilling material seems apparent, as at some of the curves the material has snapped. This, assuming it to have been heated before its insertion, is perhaps in consequence of inserting it before being sufficiently warmed, although there are present other irregularities which may be put down more as the result of hastiness.

The corners have the peculiar dug-out or indented appearance characteristic of him at all times, but not to the same degree, as there are instances where two or three corners have this impress of the maker, while the fourth may have very little trace of it, this perhaps being likewise the result of hurry to get finished.

Another specimen made, I have no doubt, about the same period, presents altogether different features with

F2

regard to outline or modelling.　It gives no impression

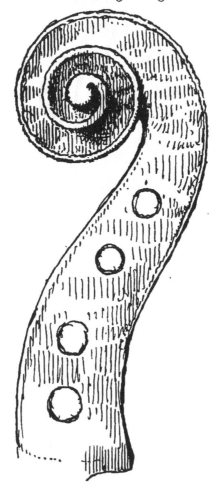

SCROLL OF JOSEPH GUARNERIUS,
1714.

at first of having anything in common with Joseph

Guarnerius or Andreas Gisalberti. The size also is larger than we are accustomed to see with either. Being placed before me with the upper table loose, I was further surprised at the presence of a ticket, written in the quaint half print, half writing style of Andreas Gisalberti, which was as follows :—

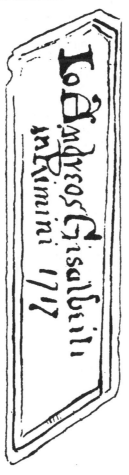

This ticket was placed in an unusual position, one which could not be better selected for being imperceptible to the ordinary observer, on the back, close to the lining on the right side just below the lower right corner. The paper had been cut to the ink lines, which were meant for a border and fitted to the place. There had been no disturbance of this ticket, as when the corner was lifted the original clean surface of the wood was exposed.

The rise of the arching, back and front, was more pronounced than that known to me during any of Joseph's periods; it was also different in the arrangement and proportion of the curves. On closer examination of details one thing was certain, that the purfling was Joseph's and no other; it was broad and bold enough for a large sized viola or even violoncello, hastily inserted all round in his own manner, and in this respect so like the 1714 violin that it seemed as if done on the same day; the material was likewise identical. Of the pine, beyond the fact of its being of high class, nothing can be said, but the sycamore was apparently from the same tree as the smaller violin of Mr. Hewett's; this, of good nutmeggy grain, gave the impression of being a plain portion of an otherwise richly curled log. The varnish was of good quality but different from Gisalberti's usual varnish. The scroll was seemingly an attempt at greater neatness than usual, but consistent with the work of Gisalberti. Taking the whole contour into consideration, with the curious ff, the conclusion seemed most reasonable that the violin was firstly designed and built upon the block or mould by Gisalberti, and the remaining work completed by Joseph. The ff are a curious mixture of Gasparo da Salo and Amati, and are Gisalberti's.

This may have been suggested by the presence among the belongings of Gisalberti of some work of his Pesaro friends.

There will be still remaining the mystery of this violin being signed and possibly disposed of as the work of Andreas Gisalberti when he had retired to Rimini.

The treatment of the scroll is more in agreement with the work of Gisalberti, although much opposed to the type put forward by him at Bozzolo in the same year. The ribs and interior linings are in the style of Gisalberti.

·CHAPTER VIII.

JOSEPH'S PECULIARITY OF HANDIWORK IN DETAIL, THE
MODELLING, ff, AND THE NICKS—HIS AND HIS
TEACHER'S HEADS, WITH THE VOLUTES OR TURNS
—THE FREE GOUGING OF THEM—THE PEG BOX—
HEIGHT OF RIBS.

A WELL known feature among the details and
minutiæ of Joseph's peculiar handiwork, and
present in both of the last two mentioned violins,
has been imitated by succeeding makers and copyists without number. The imitators are very careful to make their
copies complete with this touch of handiwork. This is
looked for as a mark of positive identity by many people,
overlooking the fact that these points, interesting as they
may be to the moderns, were in all probability at the
time of their make, almost matters of accident resulting
chiefly from habits connected with haste, and a manner
of working the parts that had descended from his master;
it is a very slight alteration from an almost constant
mannerism in Gisalbert's work.

With the latter, the indentation seems to have been
done by a small tool, perhaps a file, being worked from
the outward but middle part of the corner in direct
opposition to the point or mitreing. The indentation by
Joseph Guarnerius has more of the appearance of direct
downward pressure, or as if stamped just after the
insertion.

It has nearly always an unevenness, as if impetuously
done on the thought of the moment, and is as a general

rule more emphatic in those instruments belonging to his boldly worked type.

As concerning the small peg so often seen at the upper and lower part of the back of violins by most of the Italian schools at this period, Joseph does not appear to have inserted any. The use of this small matter of detail has often been discussed; the most probable reason seems to be that some makers placed the back in position while attending to some of the finishing of the form or border, and the peg would enable them to replace the back and register correctly. The modelling is of gentle rise from the border, what there is of channelling or grooving being very little if at all below the level of the outer edge of the purfling. This peculiarity or system, seems to have been fairly constant with him during his working career. There is, in consequence of the very gradual rise toward the middle, an appearance of flatness which is more prolonged at each end. If the exact height of the apex of the arching be measured above the level plane, it will be found to be about the same as a medium model of Stradivari; the latter would seem more full to the eye in consequence of the arching commencing nearer to the purfling.

Now as to the sound holes, as will be seen by reference to the illustration, there is very little intention evident of an entire change in design from the Gisalberti type; effort seems present at improvement only, no radical alteration being meant. They are both placed upright, the lower holes are not quite so large, the strangely determined curl of the lower wing is checked in its course and the upper hole drilled slightly larger, the nicks are kept rather low down and more modest in size. Both upper and lower wings are kept nearly an eighth of an inch away from the opposing curve, the lower one being also much narrower than the earlier type of 1706.

The scroll, freely carved, is well conceived, the first turn, as with his teacher's heads, being rather high up, the back grooves not very deeply gouged, the shell of medium depth and of average width. Here, there is a

distinct departure from the Gisalberti style, as there is
more emphatic hollowing out each side of the centre
line.　As is often the case with his middle and late
periods, there is perceptible the working of the gouge
upwards and downwards to avoid the tearing of the
fibres of the wood and the meeting place where the
grain runs more level is not quite smoothed down.　In
the manner of gouging, Joseph, by his absence of finely
levelled surface, gives us some inkling of his manner of
gouging, the tool not going round and following the turns
as so many makers have done, but nearly across from
left to right and from right to left, thus only reversing the
scroll once for one or the other side.　This would be in
agreement with the hypothesis that with all the freedom,
hurry, haphazard method and carelessness that critics
have laid to his charge, there was the greatest probability
that Joseph carefully traced the pattern on to the wood
before any gouging was proceeded with.　To do without
this would invite disaster even with Joseph's genius
trebled; it is even very doubtful whether with his mode of
carving this part it could be done at all without the guide
lines.　The specimen under consideration has further
points of interest connected with the carving of the
scroll which should be noticed, the "ear," as it is
generally termed among connoisseurs, giving some indication of that emphatic or impetuous touch of the gouge
where the first or smallest turn begins; this is generally
looked upon as a touch given by haste or accident rather
than anything else.　There is a more important detail in
the carrying out of the design which is seen when looking
at the back of the head, that is the shelving down of the
edge of the turn soon or at once after it leaves the axis
or "eye."　This is observable on all the scrolls of Gisalberti that have come under my notice.

Joseph Guarnerius, uncertain artist as he was in the
treatment of the next instrument after the last that had
left his hands, was, as a general rule, steadfast in his
retention of this peculiarity of detail; although I have
seen some exceptions to this, in which there seemed to

be a determination to go opposite in that respect to the course to which he had been always accustomed.

The peg box is roomy right up to the part under the volute, which is not much hollowed out, but seeming as if sufficient for the purpose in the eyes of Joseph. Very few makers of the Cremonese school continued the grooving at the underneath as emphatically as the more exposed portions. Even the Amatis and Stradivari left it a trifle more shallow, although well finished.

The edges of the turns of the scroll are squared, but not coarsely—not as boldly as might be expected with such a border and purfling.

There does not appear to be any particular effort at expression in the set or posing of the head over the peg box, although there is sufficient firmness of intention to make a harmonious design.

With regard to the modelling in general of the upper and lower tables, there is much that is interesting when these important particulars are considered in detail. Although, taken as a whole, the modelling is at once evident as belonging to the "flat" style, that is, with very slight elevation at the highest point, yet it cannot be said to be less elaborate than a highly vaulted one—on the contrary, there is present a perceptibly strong indication that the maker was working under the impression that the model of low elevation required more attention if possible than the one of medium height.

In the systematic gouging we can see the difference of intention between Joseph Guarnerius and Gasparo da Salo in the management of their tools over their flatter modellings. In the former, the use of a broad gouge is noticeable each side at the waist, the outer edge of the tool resting just inside the border, where running along until a trifle beyond the corner, the stroke or push of the tool is checked and the channel comes almost to a full stop, or, as it may be termed, blends with the other curves in close proximity.

With Gasparo da Salo the gouge is thrust along further some distance towards the middle of the upper quarter, and the same at the lower one; a smaller gouge then carries the channellings round continuously with the border. This mannerism was followed very frequently by Gisalberti, more particularly in his higher vaulted modellings than his low pitched ones, and appears to be good evidence that the different makers of the day studied closely what had been done before their time as well as that which was going on around them, not only of their own school but those of opposite tastes and tendencies.

Antonio Mariani with one gouge ran the channelling all round with apparently the same tool. Thus, although aiming at a general effect not very dissimilar to that of Gasparo, the means for obtaining the end are more akin to those of Giovanni Paolo Maggini during his middle and late periods.

Thus it will be perceptible that Joseph Guarnerius, although adopting at so early a period a system of flat modelling, did not resort to an imitation of the manner of any of the Brescian masters, but was anxious to adopt a method of gouging peculiarly his own. Doubtless he was acquainted with the mannerisms of most of the Brescian makers, and the Pesaro branch in particular from which his master, Gisalberti came. There were, as a matter of course, many specimens of all the makers now known to us constantly coming under his notice, and also of a great many more who had a reputation then, and whose names are lost to us now, perhaps never to be recovered.

At the upper and lower ends the curving or gouging is flatter—necessarily so, if harmony and consistency of treatment were to be guiding rules. There is, as must naturally follow, much less or scarcely any channelling.

The junction of the ribs at the corners is effected in the manner of Gisalberti, that is, without the edge being squared off in the manner of Stradivari and some of his pupils.

The original height of the ribs is always a difficult matter to estimate satisfactorily unless an instrument comes down to us in almost absolute virgin purity. This is owing to the bad habits and rough treatment of non-mechanical people who will persist in meddling with work that ought to be attended to solely by experienced hands. The violin being somewhat out of order, the interior is supposed to be in need of examination if not of repair; all the same it is opened very frequently in the most haphazard or ruffianly manner, with the result that both upper table and ribs at the part of attachment are torn about in different directions, and then to make matters worse, the surfaces are planed down so as to fit better, as is supposed. So often is evidence present of this process having been gone through that very few indeed of the violins in supposed almost pristine condition have their original full height of ribs.

With regard to the varnish, there is some slight indication of an effort at enrichment of the material in use; the low toned yellow—assuming it to have been generally used by Joseph in his early days—though of this we cannot be quite sure—is succeeded by a warm brown, very thinly laid in most parts, especially about the upper table. It is more thickly or roughly laid about the head and parts of the ribs and lower table; where it is so, the surface is frizzled, as is the case with so many of the softly varnished instruments of the Italian masters.

The quality is more oily in general appearance than the yellow of former years; it may, however, be only a little different from the other in consequence of a slight change in the preparation before application. The under coating is clear, and of apparently the ordinary Cremonese material used at the time, serving well the purpose, among others, of keeping the upper film of varnish, which is more charged with colour, from sinking and marring the clear view of the fibres. The frizzled appearance of the varnish in the least handled parts of the instrument may be the result of dryness, perhaps combined with warmth, that has contracted the upper portion more rapidly than the lower.

There is much yet to be learnt concerning the different ways of drying or ageing of varnish under various conditions ; the manner of contraction frequently giving out a hint as to the component materials used either as a basis or for colouring.

Of the necessity for a properly prepared surface on which to place his varnish, Joseph Guarnerius seems to have been quite aware. What this particular preparation consisted of has been always a puzzle to connoisseurs, who have not yet been able to leave the regions of perplexity.

CHAPTER IX.

FURTHER REFERENCE TO THE TICKETS OF GISALBERTI
WHEN HE WAS STAYING AT BOZZOLO—HIS VIOLINS
MADE TO SUIT HIS PATRONS THERE—HIS WOOD AND
INTERIOR WORK—THE OCCASIONAL CONFUSION OF
JOSEPH WITH GISALBERTI—THE TONE PECULI-
ARITIES OF EITHER—DIFFERENT PLACES WHERE
GISALBERTI WORKED—HIS MAKING OF VIOLON-
CELLOS.

WE will now take up the continuation of our study
of the works of Joseph's teacher, and to begin
with, we here produce a facsimile of another
of Andrea Gisalberti's tickets, to which previous reference has been made.

The peculiar rough manner of writing inside the
quaint loose suggestion of an ornamental border, executed on the spur of the moment, will be recognised as
being so like the Ballarini ticket of Rimini many years
later.

From the fact of the ticket being written and not

printed as the 1716 one of Parma, we may infer that it
was not Gisalberti's intention to permanently reside at
Bozzolo, or that he was at all certain about the length
of his stay there. The question of cost of block, and
printing of many tickets from it, would as naturally be a
matter for consideration with him as with any maker of
the present time.

On this ticket we have a most important piece of
evidence in support of the conjecture put forward in an
earlier chapter that Andreas Gisalberti, as referred to
on the tickets of his pupil Joseph Guarnerius, was in all
probability working for some time at Cremona, and well
known there among the devotees of the art of violin
playing. That there are tickets still extant having some
reference to the place I have felt sure, even in spite of
the destructive agencies which have for so long been at
work, accompanied by good or evil intention ; the good
intention going hand in hand with ignorance, the evil
with avarice.

Here is a ticket, however, which is the strongest
evidence possible—that of Gisalberti's own assertion
before his patrons of Bozzolo—that he was known
as that of Cremona, or, as we may take it, had been
working and was best known there. The violins of
Gisalberti made at Bozzolo, judging by two that have
come before me (another has been described as having
precisely similar characteristics), form a distinct sub-type,
and might be termed his Bozzolo period.

The cause of there being to a limited extent a distinct-
ness of character marked over the instruments made at
that place, may be fairly put down to the operation of the
law of supply and demand.

An artist, musician, actor, or writer, does not concen-
trate his energies upon producing that which he is certain
will never be wanted : he believes in his power of being
able to supply that which is really required, and for
which he sees there is, or soon will be, a brisk demand.
He often sees too, that a little change from his usual
manner will prove satisfactory to his patrons, and there-

fore advantageous to himself. We may thus argue that at Bozzolo, violins of a moderate rise in the arching were mostly preferred, and that in his modelling he conformed to the tastes or fancies of the people in the locality.

His patrons seem, however, to have been quite content with his quaint management of the outline, this varying, but still being unopposed in style to those associated with his name, although made at other places.

In those of the Bozzolo period the border is broad, the purfling not so massive: he may have had some slight leanings towards a possible delicacy of treatment in this matter of detail; it is not evenly inserted, varying in thickness at parts; now and then, as one looks round, there is a portion executed with a neatness unsurpass-able, followed by a part showing uncertainty or even a tendency to raggedness. Gisalberti was certainly not gifted with the steady iron-nerve-like capacity of Stradivari in this direction. Two more opposite men in mental constitution could not perhaps possibly be.

Gisalberti's pupil, Joseph Guarnerius, with all his variation in mode and humour of working, seems never to have looked upon the even, firm, determined line of Stradivari with much admiration; it is very seldom indeed that his work in all details can be placed in fair comparison with, or likened to, that of the very conserva-tive master.

In common with almost all the foremost members of the Italian fraternity of liutaros, Gisalberti constantly varied his pattern or outline, possibly according to the humour of the moment. We thus find that with him, notwithstanding a determined quaintness of manner natural to him, and from which he seems never to have tried to sever himself, he yet found it possible to give variety, without which he would have proved himself deficient in one of the great essentials of Italian art, and one of the most prominent characteristics of each of the great masters.

These Bozzolo violins have all the other peculiarities of Gisalberti present, if we except that of the posing of the sound holes. These, which it will be observed are different on the Rimini and Parma specimens, are placed more in the manner usual among Cremonese makers of the time, that is, with what is known as some amount of flow, and not with the upper part leaning back towards the border. He did on rare occasions, possibly to please someone, incline them very much toward the centre, quite in a reverse manner to that on the majority of his designs.

A few words on this point. The inclination of the upper portion of the sound holes outwardly or toward the border was not a singularily of Gisalberti; on the contrary, many of the Italian makers occasionally gave way to this freak of fancy. It is by no means certain, either, that the masters of the art, their patrons, looked upon the setting or posing of the sound holes of a violin from the same standpoint as we do now. At the present time connoisseurs are in the habit of looking upon a violin almost invariably in the same manner, it is taken up and looked at with the head upright ; all parts receding from it and below are expected, in orthodox fashion, to get larger and bolder. This will do very well until a master-piece turns up with this regularity of progressive form apparently set at defiance ; the piece may be looked upon as an eccentricity and not as a classical model, in conse-quence of the breach of some unwritten law of which no person is cognisant at the present day, but which was probably in operation in the olden times.

Every design must be judged by the beauty of line and harmony of proportion contained within itself.

Critics of sound judgment will not place a violin in an inferior rank to that of one of the great masters because it has not been conceived or carried out in the same spirit.

A maker of originality may fix upon a combination of form and proportion with a most happy result, quite different from, or even opposed to, the ideas assumed to be manifested in the works of the Raphael of violin construction. It is within the bounds of possibility to differ from him in conception of the combined beauties which he brought together, while at the same time producing a result having the stamp of highest excellence upon it.

Many beautiful designs by makers not yet acknowledged to be in the first rank have thus appeared at times, circumstances being very favourable for allowing the man to unfold before the eyes of the world the wealth of power that was innate within him.

As an instance the Mantua maker, Balestrieri, may be referred to ; the public generally know of him as a rough although characteristic maker, but on convenient occasion, or when allowed, he could manifest his powers as an artist of a very high degree of talent.

Gisalberti's eccentricities in placing the sound holes may not have seemed so much out of the way when his violins first made their appearance, but the leaning back of the upper portion, being a well defined fancy of his, was a prominent feature at most times.

In the violin with the Parma ticket of 1716 there is the distinct widening out of the space between the upper part of the sound holes; afterwards, when he had retired to Pesaro, he sent forth other patterns of like peculiarities—perhaps many more than we at present know of—but in the intermediate or Bozzolo specimens there is seemingly an effort at conforming with the tastes or requirements of the locality by placing the sound holes more vertical, or with the upper holes closer in.

This, combined with less rise in the modelling may, I think, be taken as fair evidence of a desire to please his patrons; his varnish is of deeper colour than those hitherto met with belonging to Parma or Pesaro. There can be very little doubt that he could have imparted a more intense hue to his varnish had he felt inclined to do so, but there is still shown a desire to keep to a modest appearance rather than any approach to gaudiness.

His sycamore is of the finest quality, as in all the other specimens known. Surely he must have taken to each place on route a large stock of this quality, it is so

G2

much alike, with the broad curl mostly arranged so as to decline from each side of the central joint of the back, and it has its full complement of what are known as the nutmeggy marks.

The pine used, although having the appearance of first-class material, varies in the width of thread; the trees probably had not the obliging quality of growing the rings with such regularity or closeness as would please all modern connoisseurs. Of the tone, however, every person who hears the Gisalberti instruments recognises it as of the highest class, and suitable for great performers.

Of the interior work, the same must be said of it as of the rest; the linings are broad strips of pine not let into the blocks, but the latter are cut away slightly at an angle where the lining is attached, so that the upper and lower corner blocks present the appearance of an octagon roughly drawn.

The inner surfaces of the upper and lower tables do not present the roughness which we might expect after looking at the other details of workmanship, and it is in this matter that we are led to reflect upon the meaning or cause of the rugged appearance of the whole, and to come to the conclusion that it was not resultant upon haste or carelessness, but was a peculiarity of style or mannerism. There seems to have been always what dealers call "plenty of wood," the backs being very robust, and in one instance, at least, that I know of, about a quarter of an inch in thickness about the centre.

This calls to mind a remark in the work of Fétis that the early works of Joseph Guarnerius were made too thick in the back, and the possibility suggests itself that the writer, or his informant, may have seen a Gisalberti and thought it to be a Joseph Guarnerius.

Indeed, there appears to be much probability that a number of Gisalberti's violins without their original tickets have passed, for long generations perhaps, without a suspicion on the part of their owners, or many of the connoisseurs and dealers who may have come into contact with them, that these violins were made by other hands than those of the renowned Joseph Guarnerius, of Cremona.

Let us think for a moment how these instruments may have appeared to the eyes of intending purchasers of old masters: a selected number of violins being produced of various styles and with different degrees of finish, were offered, frequently in good faith, by the vendors, and as lawyers sometimes put it, according to the best of their knowledge and belief, that the particular specimens were genuine and even typical of the master whose work they had too readily assumed them to be, in total absence of knowledge of any such maker as Andreas Gisalberti having lived. The rugged aspect, apparently hasty execution, often uneven insertion of the purfling, curiously free drawing of the sound holes, the fine quality of the pine, excellent figure of the sycamore, not omitting the boldly and sometimes finely designed scroll —these, with the pellucid varnish, would be referred to as very strong evidence against any disputant.

If more evidence were deemed necessary to support the foregoing, it would supposititously be supplied by the style of drawing adopted for the waist curves. The invariable shortness of these (so far as my knowledge goes) would not be considered as of much account by one whose wish was father to the thought in the matter; the principal feature in the design of this part by Gisalberti being the frequent large sweep of line at the upper part, so distinct from and opposite to anything seen in the work of Stradivari, or of the Amatis. It is quite within the bounds of possibility that Joseph Guarnerius, having this peculiarity of design constantly before him while being reared in the art of designing and constructing violins, had come to look upon it as a canon or necessary law to follow in precedence to any other, and, retaining the influence to a more or less degree during the whole of his career, was indisposed to make any wide departure from the pet fancy of his teacher, but rather to extend or develop the idea. This would be quite in accordance with the usual way, or disposition of the pupil, to walk in the footsteps of his master until the powers and peculiarities innate with him have progressively become more potent, until too strong for restraint.

With regard to the tone of the Gisalbertis that may have been sold at times as the work of Joseph Guarnerius, there would be little or no difficulty on the part of the vendor of the former, the quality in all respects being much the same with both masters, although both of them, in common with other masters, sent forth instruments varying in the volume of their tone as well as in some minor particulars. A few words may be added concerning the carving of the scrolls of Gisalberti's violins. That he was a man of variable humour has before been stated, but the striking difference between the violins of the Parma, Rimini, and Bozzolo periods can only be accounted for on the supposition, as before put forward, that at the latter place Gisalberti found it necessary to conform to the whims or prejudices of the people who purchased from or commissioned him.

The Bozzolo type of head is a really fine production, with a rather delicately formed peg-box, the scroll having bold turns and looking rather narrow from the front.

The grooves running down from the back part of the scroll to what is known as the shell, in those specimens that have come under my notice, have had much the same handling, in each instance there being an evident indisposition to carve much of a hollow on each side of the central line ; in this respect he differs from his great pupil Joseph, who one day would carve this part in a manner strongly suggestive of his master, and the next time be very emphatic in the hollowing of the shell, so much so as to cause the connoisseur of moderate experience to have some doubts for a moment as to the identity of the maker, or of a later possible interference by some repairer or improver.

The size of the scrolls cut by Gisalberti at different times and in different localities vary much, and might suggest to a casual observer the work of two different men, rather than of one who seemed to be swayed about by conflicting influences, or by his own capriciousness. On close scrutiny and comparison between different specimens there will be seen some signs remaining of the method of working, and even of the marking or tracing down on to the wood of the guiding lines for gouging; there is very little however, in fact not so much as may be sometimes seen on the work of those masters of elegance and finish, the Amati family. The gouging is always of an apparently hasty kind, with little or none of the polishing up afterwards of the edges of each turn, such as is so often seen with less vigorous workmanship. In this department of work Gisalberti seems to have had no fixed intention of keeping to a well set type, a good boldness and effectiveness seem to have been the prevailing ideas; all small niggling work must have been an abhorrence to him, and he would have none of it.

It was apparently this spirit that animated him while turning out the probably great number of quaintly formed violins, some violas—of basses he probably made but few—which in hands more accustomed to very delicate knife work would have been made more attractive to the eye of the average admirer of the Italian liutaro's art.

Like many others—his contemporaries perhaps among them; it may have been more like a general rule than would at first be suspected—he seems to have decided upon a certain type for the time being, keeping fairly within certain boundaries of what he found, either by observation or direct request, was a necessity in the pursuit of success in gaining favour among likely patrons at Bozzolo. This supposition is helped by the fact of his return to his own particular fancy in the treatment of his work after leaving this place.

He appears to have been at Bozzolo about one year, and then removed to Rimini. It has been stated that he worked at other places than Cremona, Parma and Bozzolo before—as it would appear by date—finally settling at Rimini.

This was probably his last place of working. I have been informed that his latest tickets have the date of 1740, when (if this be true), he was probably an aged man.

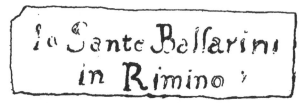

Late ticket of Sante Ballarini (Andreas Gisalberti); may not have been dated, probably made between 1730 and 1734. An illustration of Mr. Hewett's viola gives a good idea of the late style of Andreas Gisalberti. (*See Plates XVI. and XVII.*)

From the want of knowledge outside Italy, and especially in Great Britain, till recently, of even the existence of an old Italian violin maker with the name of Andreas Gisalberti, or the alias Sante Ballarini, it is strongly probable that from the land of their birth many well preserved specimens by the master—for to this title he has the strongest claim—may yet emerge, perhaps to please more highly those whose tastes have not been formed on a sufficiently broad basis to acknowledge as an artist of very high rank one whose peculiarities of style would appear to them as too eccentric.

In reviewing the work of Andreas Gisalberti as a whole, that is, so far as the limited number of instruments which have turned up will allow, a question will naturally arise as to his rightful position in the future among the masters of his craft. That he cannot claim a very high position among the great ones with regard to refinement in form is indisputable; beyond possessing a certain kind of native intuition in designing his different patterns he seems to have had no desire to become conspicuous by the elegance of his productions, indeed the term beauty of form may have been to him but an empty expression and with which he had no desire for acquaintance. Exquisite form therefore must be left out of the category of necessary attributes of a fine violin if he is to be permitted to contend for the pride of place.

Fine form and beauty in detail being placed aside as unnecessary adjuncts in completing the work upon which he set out, he seems to have trusted, as regards workmanship, to what is known among connoisseurs everywhere as "character," a term synonymous with sufficiently marked individuality of manner in both designing and constructing. In this direction he was very powerful, and by some people might be thought to have been so much so as to be on the verge of offensiveness, but to this point very few would be bold enough to say he ever reached. He kept steadily orthodox in his retention and strict observance of the proportion of the various details to the whole, and which was firstly demonstrated in the works of the great master of Brescia, Gasparo da Salo, and held by his pupils, and followed as a sort of canon to be always held in respect and obedience.

Next, in the matter of varnishing, he can not only hold his own well, but demands recognition as a master who had been thoroughly initiated into the secrets of the envelopment of his work with what we may term those mysterious ingredients of the wonderful varnishes of his day, known to us moderns as "the old Italian varnish," which is a wrong term, as there was as much variety in the qualities of the beautiful coverings of the old Italian instruments as there is in the styles of the works themselves. Gisalberti's varnish is of a distinct type, and from his use of apparently the same essence, fusion, or whatever its component parts consisted of, he either carried with him from place to place the raw materials, or they were obtained by him where he sojourned, and made up— possibly in secret—at convenient places and times.

His varnish varying in depth of colour or intensity, is some evidence of his ability, had he called upon it, to produce some of the more showy effects obtained by other masters of the Venetian, Cremonese and Milanese

schools. There is a beautiful subdued glow in Gisalberti's unspoilt coats of varnish, combined with exceeding clearness and softness, which to many would be far
preferable to a more positive colour with risk of a charge
of gaudiness.

In criticising Gisalberti's tone as the third item,
nothing too high can be said of it. As with all other
tone masters, his violins differ in their degrees of power,
although in common with the leaders in each school the
same species of tone quality is adhered to.

Some of his violins have an extraordinary sonority,
capable in all essentials of satisfying the demands of the
most exacting soloist anxious to make his mark in a
crowded concert hall.

The wood of which he constructed his instruments has
before been referred to, but a few words may be added
about the exact similarity of his sycamore to that used
by Joseph Guarnerius up to his latest known dates.
Almost invariably handsome in curl, it has the peculiarity
of not turning to the dirty brown common to most of the
wood used by other makers of the time and various
localities. On close examination, the apparently light
colour still pervading it after such a lapse of time, is
found to be caused chiefly by the brightness or glitter of
the interstices or pores, and only by trying the wood
under different unreflected lights, will the actual local
colour be clearly discernible.

From the exactness with which the sycamore of Gisalberti agrees in all respects with that of his pupil Joseph
Guarnerius, we may fairly draw our conclusions, that not
only was the wood of both selected from the same
district, but the first in all probability informed the other
of the means or whereabouts for obtaining it. That
both used identically the same kind of tree, appreciating
its great virtues, is a fact full of interest to the connoisseur and modern maker, and if a trifle more information of the same kind could be obtained it might be the
means of opening up very important clues in other
directions.

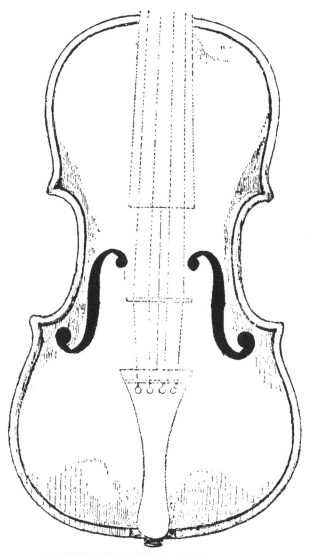

ANDREAS GISALBERTI, BOZZOLO, 1717.

The violin on the preceding page has the back in one piece, with bold curls running straight across; the sides or ribs are of the same wood. The front is of very open threaded pine, particularly at the outside, and it is in two parts. The varnish is of his usual light brown. The modelling has a very slight rise, and but little channelling. The tone is of great excellence.

Andreas Gisalberti did not confine himself to the making of violins, as it has been popularly supposed his pupil did; he made violas of full size, good work covered with his fine varnish, and emitting a beautiful tone of great volume; he also made violoncellos, as was proved by one turning up which had been travelling over many countries as a solo instrument, and carrying an increasing reputation as it went for its tone qualities.

As a matter of course—it might almost be said—the names given to it by various performers, dealers and others, who had never seen its like before, were more and more numerous and interesting as it went along; latterly a conclusion arrived at was that it was by an early Cremonese maker, a ticket, therefore, with the name was obtained and duly installed in position with the aid of some gum!

In the City of London one day this violoncello came under my notice, and proved a great surprise, as on examination I was able to certainly announce as the author, Andreas Gisalberti of Cremona, Parma, Bozzolo and Rimini, the teacher of Joseph Guarnerius.

Upon further examination there was no difficulty in perceiving the most likely causes for different names being assigned to it, the ff being of the Amati style— although cut in Gisalberti's manner—and these not seeming to agree with the workmanship, outline, gouging of the scroll, and materials, confusion inevitably followed.

Why Gisalberti cut the ff in the Amati style is a matter of conjecture, and which cannot be entered upon now with any prospect of settlement or even profit. It may have been done at the desire of the patron who wished to have the instrument made somewhat to his fancy, and who did not like the ordinary Gisalberti type which he had seen, but who wanted Gisalberti's tone.

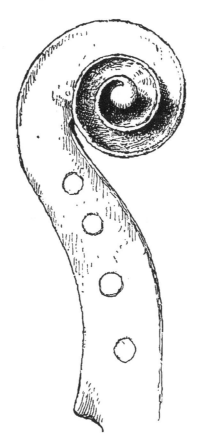

HEAD AND SCROLL OF GISALBERTI VIOLIN,
BOZZOLO PERIOD, 1717.

This violin has the back in two parts of rich figure,
the curls going upwards from the centre, the
ribs of the same wood.

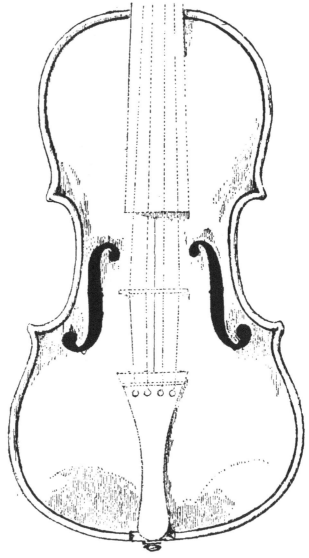

ANDREAS GISALBERTI,
CREMONENSIS FECIT IN BOZZOLO, 1717.

In this instance there is indication enough that the maker could, when required, depart from his usual line, and that his quaint, almost humorous, expression of contour and accompanying *f f* was not from inability to do otherwise. (*See Plates XVIII., XIX., XX., XXI., and XXII.*)

CHAPTER X.

THE PINE USED BY THE OLD ITALIAN MAKERS—ITS
PECULIARITIES AND TONE-PRODUCING QUALITIES
—THE STORAGE OF TIMBER BY THE MANY MAKERS
—WORM-PUNCTURED WOOD.

HAD there been any means perceptible whereby
some data, historical, or otherwise, could have
been obtained concerning the pine used by the
old Italian makers, much interesting matter might have
been added to our subject. There is strong indication of
the wood used by both master and pupils having been
cut from trees of the same genus, perhaps under the
same climatic conditions, soil and surroundings, or from
the same forest (assuming that the trees were of the kind
which grew in great numbers or were clustered together),
and even the same part of the tree.

It is but a reasonable surmise that the selection of the
exact tone-giving kind took place on the spot while the
tree was growing, not after the cutting down, and
possibly under the direction, after search, of the liutaros
or their advisers.

If we grant the likelihood of the pine having been first
cut indiscriminately by woodmen or merchants, regardless of its acoustical qualities, it would, as a matter of
course, be only so much timber to be hewn down in the
ordinary routine of business, or sold, with all faults and
errors of description, perhaps by auction, the good
sounding bits being picked out according to the judgment or whim of the purchaser.

Plate XVIII.
VIOLONCELLO, ANDREAS GISALBERTI, C. 1716.
Owned by Mr. P. A. ROBSON.

Plate XIX.
VIOLONCELLO, ANDREAS GISALBERTI, C. 1716.
Owned by Mr. P. A. ROBSON.

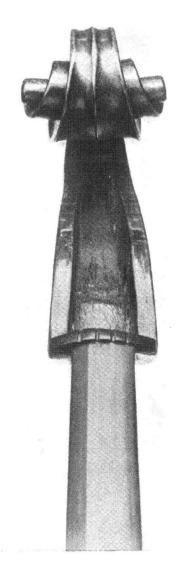

Plate XX.
VIOLONCELLO, ANDREAS GISALBERTI, C. 1716. SCROLL.
Owned by Mr. P. A. ROBSON.

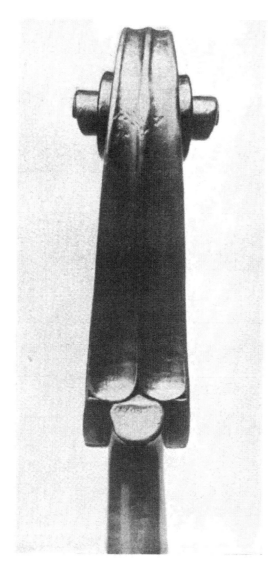

Plate XXI.
VIOLONCELLO, ANDREAS GISALBERTI, C. 1716. SCROLL.
Owned by Mr. P. A. ROBSON.

Plate XXII.
VIOLONCELLO, ANDREAS GISALBERTI, C. 1716. SCROLL.
Owned by Mr. P. A. ROBSON.

Plate XXIII.
VIOLIN, JOSEPH GUARNERIUS, 1710.
Ownd by Mr G. ROLLETT.

Plate XXIV.
VIOLIN, JOSEPH GUARNERIUS, 1710.
Owned by Mr. G. ROLLETT.

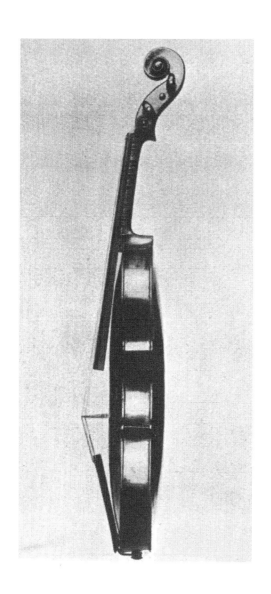

Plate XXV.
VIOLIN, JOSEPH GUARNERIUS, 1710.
Owned by Mr. G. ROLLETT.

Supposing this to have been the usual course of the business—and there must necessarily have been a very large number of commercial transactions going on in acquiring pine for musical instruments generally—then discrimination of proper quality by the eye was the general system in vogue for obtaining suitable material.

That the pine was not taken at random, or merely for its pleasing aspect, there is much evidence, and no very lengthened experience is necessary to perceive this.

The fact of different well known masters constructing a number of instruments for which the same pine or identical tree had been chosen, speaks loudly in support of the hypothesis that it was for the acoustical quality before any other that the wood was selected.

The use of a very close threaded piece of pine for one instrument and a piece quite the reverse in another, is further indication that the quality of tone desired being the same in both, was not dependent upon what could be seen by the eye.

Again, occasionally instruments may be met with having the upper table made from three or even four pieces, when, if appearance was the desideratum, enough wood of straight fibre might have been found of sufficient width for an upper table in one or two pieces only.

Further, some very fine or even famous instruments have been seen having the upper table made from pine inclined to, or much affected with, knottiness. Instances have come under my own observation of violins by Stradivari and the Amatis having this peculiarity. It is, perhaps, more frequently seen with basses than the smaller instruments, two instances occurring to my mind, in one of which, by an old Italian maker of lesser renown, three large, hard and distinctly formed knots were present. The impression made upon the thinking spectator was that of the terribly hard labour undertaken to work through these and make a good top surface. "What a job!" exclaimed one, "the maker must have thought a great deal of these pieces of pine to have hewn through those hard knots." In reply the observa-

H

tion was tendered that the maker had doubtless some means at his command by which he had ascertained that the almost unworkable plank of pine would supply the particular quality of tone which his patrons would be pleased with.   Furthermore, it is not a very rare circumstance to find pieces of various sizes inserted in the table, apparently to fill up some cavity or cast formed during the growth of the tree, the width and length of which was insufficient to allow of any avoidance.

These instances will perhaps be enough for our present purpose—that of showing the value the master liutaros of Italy must have placed upon their store of pine.   That they did store their very precious sounding material there is no lack of evidence.   It was not the pine alone which they hoarded up for future use; planks of richly figured sycamore were seemingly held back for special times when money would be forthcoming, and work of a specially handsome appearance might be called for.

The evidence in support of this is mostly seen in the works of the well known masters, which again strengthens the hypothesis that they were not, among the liutaros of their day, poor struggling artisans of a low degree of social standing.   They must necessarily have had some place which served them as a maga-zine from which they could draw forth such portions as were suitable to the requirements of the moment, or possibly the remuneration to be expected from their patrons.

That the storage did not take place in any back parlor, cellar, or attic, is probable from the fact of some of the material used in the construction of the finest specimens known, having been cut from wood that has been punc-tured by insects in parts.   The ravages of the insects— so horrifying to the connoisseur and trying to the patience of the repairer—are committed for the greater part in quite uninterfered with places, more frequently in the open air.   The liutaros of the time to which we are referring, seem to have been as well acquainted with, or it may be said troubled by, the boring of the insects as those of to-day.

With respect to the storage of the valuable timber, which may have been in the rear of the premises, perhaps some little out-house, the work of the two masters under consideration affords some interesting particulars.

We have before noticed the similarity of the pine used by the two, and this is also seen to be the case with regard to the sycamore : neither of them appears to have used any sycamore that could come under the description known among the moderns as " hard looking," meagre or "horny looking " under wear, or very plain, or wanting in curl or figure. In every instance that has come under my notice the sycamore has been of the quality recognised among connoisseurs as that of the highest class and selected from that. Some specimens, as a matter of course, are more richly figured than others, but none that have come to my knowledge have been seen with what is generally recognised as poor wood.

We have here an indication that master and pupil belonged to a good stock, or we may say, moved in the upper circles of their craft ; they were both at all times in possession of the means for obtaining the best quality of material to work upon.

In this respect the two makers compare favourably with any other two that can be taken together as working under similar circumstances.

Of the earliest makers of the Brescian school there seems to have been no exception to the rule that they were hard pushed at times for handsome or even respectable looking sycamore; frequently plum tree, pear, apple, willow and other woods, sufficiently firm in substance, and perhaps indigenous to the soil, being requisitioned. Even the Amatis, well-to-do people as supposed according to tradition, appear to have been at times lacking in the fine quality of sycamore or the means of getting it. Of the right sort of pine there does

not appear to have been a dearth, although as before
mentioned, the exact quality desired by each maker was
precious and valuable.

Considering the amount of unavoidable waste, or wood
cut away in chips and cast aside during the construction
of violins day after day during the year or season, the
quantity used from the same tree must have been very
large.   Busy with continuous work, such as without
doubt the upper classes of the Italian liutaros were
engaged in, they would, in a comparatively short time,.
perhaps a few months, dispose of quite a beam of timber.
On comparing the violins turned out from the establishments of the Amatis, Stradivaris, Guarneris, and other
equally prolific workers, one cannot help being struck
with the recurrence, in connection with each name, of
the same grain of pine, not all in one period, but at
irregular intervals.   From this we might infer that the
different makers were anxious to retain for special
occasions particular logs of pine, with the exact tone-
giving qualities of which they were, without doubt,
thoroughly acquainted.

With this view of the selection of materials for
their work, we can understand how the young Joseph
Guarnerius's violins (we are at present supposing he
confined his energies to these alone) have so close a
resemblance to those of his teacher.   For some years he
must have been content with following the footsteps of
his teacher, both in the selection of materials and the use
of them, with but little indication of the independence
that was soon to be declared.

Of this early type, Mr. George Rollit's violin, about
1710 (*See Plates XXIII., XXIV., and XXV.*) affords some
intimation of what was likely to follow, as there is more
of a distinct departure from the ways of his mentor
than in the 1706 specimen illustrated in these pages.
It will be perceptible at once where the modification
has been effected, that is, at the waist curve, or C,
the whole of which is somewhat enlarged, more particularly the lower part, which causes the corners there

to look heavier, indeed, more so than the very large majority of his numerous changes.

There is some suggestion about this pattern of his having been influenced by the other Joseph (filius Andræ) who was most likely engaged in a settled business in Cremona, but I doubt whether this, from the natural independence of Joseph, was more than an accidental approach to a type that had been put forth by this great master of varnishing. There is, however, the fact which must not be overlooked—of the *ff* being placed lower down, as was usual with his namesake.

The modelling is in agreement with the earlier or 1706 type, and in detail the tooling may be said to be of a precisely similar character.

The soundholes have unfortunately suffered a little under the hands of some member of the repairing faculty (probably long since deceased), seized with a desire to make them more Joseph-like and proper, an instance in harmony with some would-be improvements on the masters of musical composition by publishing firms in " touching up the old 'un," but in the present case it is " touching up the young 'un."

The varnish is still of the yellow or light orange colour. The scroll shows a more distinct departure from the earlier or Gisalberti time, in having a lighter character with more slender throat. The grooves at the back are gouged in a more emphatic manner, but are not of high finish. The characteristic quality of tone is maintained, and may be fairly classed as of the highest rank and charm, with a sufficiency of energy.

This violin was, in my most careful estimation, made about the year 1710, when Joseph was twenty-seven years of age.

Between this date and the violin made in 1714, referred to before, there was ample time for changes of almost any kind to have occurred. The indications thrown out in the 1710 one during this interval seem to have become more and more strong under the spirit of independence within the maker, and the aspect of this

work is such that more than a mere glance is necessary
to enable us to recognise the author.

There he is, however, with his master's influence still
present, which he has not yet thrown completely aside,
some of it never to be evaded. The pattern or outline is
quite novel, the modelling flatter, more in system than
reality, and the whole work remarkably bold. There is
another item of interest, that of its being to my knowledge the first instance of the use for the upper table of
the pine with the two lines of shade, one on each side of
the fingerboard, and running the whole length of the
table. It is sometimes called a cloud, at others a stain ;
it is a natural discoloration, less distinct in some
instances than others.

A cloud, stain, grey discoloration, or whatever it may
be called, of this kind is not rare among the old Italian
violins, having been seen in the pine tables of several
other makers of note, and therefore the mere presence of
a similar mark will be no indication of authenticity or
even locality of make ; it must be accompanied by the
exact peculiarity of grain in Joseph's wood. It is so
faint in many instances as to necessitate moving the
instrument about in the light in order to see it ; in one or
two I have found the same tree, but without this mark,
which seems not to have extended all round, possibly only
on one side, facing a particular point of the compass, and
may have been on the side least exposed to the rays of
the sun or not. It is certain that Joseph Guarnerius
retained a quantity of the wood from this precious
pine tree, from which store he took now and then as
occasion prompted him. That he thought much of it is
evidenced by the fact of some of his finest works
showing its presence, and that the stock at the first was
large is declared by the fact of his having drawn from
this quantity from 1714 till the year 1742, or possibly
later.

Compared with some of the other pine used by Joseph,
it is less regular in the gradation of the fibres or threads.
To the eyes of connoisseurs on the look-out for regularity

or mechanical sequence as being a desideratum in the combination of qualities, the pine may appear less pretty. This inequality of distance between the threads, although having a decreasing average from the border toward the centre, seems to have nothing whatever to do with the difference of quality or strength of the tone.

Much emphasis has been placed by many critical writers on the assumed superiority of a fine, straight run of thread for the production or accompanying of a fine quality of tone in a violin; some have pinned their faith on the necessity of an entire absence of any irregularity in the course of the thread, insisting that the wood should be cut far from any knots or twist in the fibres, and that these must be very fine, upright, or at right angles with the plane of the instrument.

Others have asserted their belief in a rather open or wide apart thread, and will refer to instances of remarkably fine tone accompanying this condition or appearance.

Not a few have attributed the peculiarities of tone belonging to the violins of Joseph Guarnerius to the difference caused by the presence of the cloud or stain, being apparently under the impression that the master always used wood of this particular growth.

Others have insisted on density with corresponding weight, or sufficient toughness, or that there must be perfect freedom from resin, or that it must have sufficient left in it.

These are some of the reasons put forward as indicative of the guiding lines which Joseph Guarnerius, and most likely all the leading lights of the art, kept steadfastly within view.

Very little discernment is necessary for grasping the fact that these writers and critics have fallen into the very common error of arguing upon insufficient premises. In the eager search after facts, small or great, that may be likely to open up knowledge and bring fresh principles to light, the significance of details is apt to be exaggerated, more especially when, as under the circumstances surrounding the consideration of our present subject, there is some amount of difficulty in making the necessary careful comparisons.

All of the before mentioned items, taken erroneously or not into calculation by critics of the early part of last century, must have appeared to them as containing much more force than they would at the present day, inasmuch as there was then a power of selection not at all possible now; consequently those that pleased the eye most in respect of the texture, figure or delicacy of fibre in the materials used, were preferably purchased.

Later on, when more and more of the work of each master became sought after, selection became increasingly difficult, as each specimen rose in value; condition or state of preservation became in the main the standard of value, and those which had been refused before were now snatched at with avidity.

When under the ordeal of trial by various performers, the essential qualities of tone, beauty of form and splendour of varnish were found to be on an equality with those which had arrived in times gone by, the differences, aspect of the grain, or, as was supposed by some, defects in the choice of wood, were overlooked, and the critics had to settle down to the conclusion that the makers had some good or sound reason for using material destined to be condemned by a few people in an after age, and who, literally speaking, knew nothing of the subject they were talking so loudly over. At the time it would not have been at all out of the way to hear one writer decrying Joseph's use of timber with the "cloud" as being what modern builders call "sappy" through carelessness, like, as they supposed, the other peculiarities were that he indulged in.

The same objection would, as a matter of course, not hold good where Joseph used a portion of wood that had been worm-eaten, as there is ample evidence to hand that he considered the material far too valuable to throw aside, and filled the perforated parts here and there with fresh wood, very neatly inserted even to the eyes of a modern repairer.

We may, therefore, take it as settled conclusively that the wood, with the " cloud," " shade," or stain—whichever may be thought the best description—was selected by Joseph Guarnerius with no other purpose in view than that of securing the speciality of tone which he thought better than any other for certain purposes, and which pleased the particular class of patrons by whom he had been favoured with commissions.

The lesser of the two violins illustrated (*See Plates XIII., XIV., and XV.*), of the period between 1714 and 1717—is interesting in several respects, that of evenness of thread in the pine in particular having the appearance of a selected portion of a table or plank of large size.

We have here another of those sudden changes in the treatment of some of the matters of detail, and with which Joseph's name is in the minds of many principally associated.

The difference between this type and the one of 1714, although so striking at first sight, is really not so great when carefully considered. If we could suppose the 1714 pattern to be placed in the hands of one of the old Cremonese liutaros, whose absorbing ideas of beauty in form were inseparably connected with extreme delicacy of treatment, this pattern is just what we might expect as a result of his interpretation or effort to idealize.

The proportions as a whole are retained almost in a strict sense, the corners are lengthened to a slight degree, while the curves are drawn with much more steadiness; an increase being thus gained in delicacy of appearance generally.

The size of the violin being less than the other (1714, full size), we naturally expect to find a narrower border combined with thinner corners. We are not disappointed, as we find these latter drawn out with much care and tenderness.

As to the purfling, there is a change which can only be described as remarkable, no hint has been thrown out before—we can only speak of those that have come

under personal observation—and such an alteration in
the material used is somewhat startling, as we are met
with a dark outside material, which may be ebony, with
the usual white centre; but the way in which it goes into
each corner is just his own. We may safely presume,
after examination in detail, that in constructing such a
tenderly drawn pattern, an extra effort at artistic effect
was made by the artist, possibly for some lady player
who had asked Joseph to make a nice looking violin, and
to endow it with the excellent tone which was very
likely becoming well known and associated with his
name.

Concerning the modelling as compared with the 1714,
there is very little change; in this respect, however, he
has shown his resolve to have nothing more of Gisalberti's influence over his violins, and so far as my knowledge leads me to believe, it never appeared again in any
important details. The rise from the purfling is very
gradual, with little or no channelling to the apex of the
curve or vaulting, which treatment causes an appearance
of more breadth in the design.

This is, further, more favourable to the lasting quality,
although it may not have been much in contemplation
by the designer, but looked upon from a purely artistic
point. The term "lasting quality" will be understood to
mean chiefly the retention of form under usage and
liability to injury, and survival therefrom in the hands
of competent repairers. That much attention was paid
to this part of the subject from the youth upwards of the
violin, will be perfectly clear to the student who will look
upon the growth of style in construction during the first
two centuries of its existence. It may almost in fact be
viewed as a prolonged effort at combining beautiful form
with as much durability or strength of constitution as was
consistent with other requisite conditions.

That these latter were fully taken into consideration by
Joseph Guarnerius everything bearing upon the subject
proves very distinctly, and that so far from being an
eccentric artist with untrammelled tendencies, he was,

on the contrary, of thoughtful, earnest disposition and intellectual activity.

During the period now engaging our attention, there is sufficient indication given as to what was possible in the future.

There is present, perhaps for the first time, an inkling of the open, bold and firm swing of line at the waist, coupled with the fullest part being placed above the central portion, giving what might be thought a hint of a desire to go in opposition to what was being done every day around him, and which was not in accordance with his natural tendencies, artistically considered.

The conception had occurred in a somewhat rude or rugged manner to early makers of the Brescian school, but in such a way as might lead us to think it anything but the outcome of carefully-calculated efforts and repeated trials. The artist seems to have been intellectually alive to all the variations of type introduced by contemporaries and deceased makers, and was doubtless carried onward by an intense determination to introduce something in design that had not been done before, but it was not yet mature within him—further trials were necessary.

CHAPTER XI.

JOSEPH'S EFFORTS AT IMPROVEMENT IN DESIGN—HIS
IDEAL CAREFULLY SOUGHT AFTER—WORKING ON
THE LINES OF SIMPLICITY—THE TUITION OF THE
CREMONESE MASTERS—WERE ANY SELF-TAUGHT?
—THE TEACHING OF GISALBERTI THROWN ASIDE
BY JOSEPH—PECULIARITIES OF MODELLING INTRO-
DUCED FROM TIME TO TIME—CHANGES IN VARNISH
—INCREASE OF INTENSITY OF COLOUR—ALTERA-
TION IN SYSTEM OF LININGS—INTERIOR FINISH
OF DIFFERENT MAKERS—DIFFERENCE BETWEEN
THAT OF JOSEPH AND STRADIVARI—EFFECTIVE
APPEARANCE.

NOTWITHSTANDING the changes in pattern
and modelling made by Joseph up to the time
on which our attention is centred, there will be
perceptible, on careful comparison, one prevailing idea
uppermost in the mind of the artist, that of the production of a design that would equal in gracefulness and
fine proportions any masterpiece that had been sent out
from establishments of the best standing in Cremona
of that day, or any time before; to the attainment of
this he devoted his most earnest efforts. That this was
so there are all necessary hints thrown out in the works
which have been engaging our attention up to the
present.

The ideal sought after was, in all likelihood, in a hazy
or nebulous condition in his mind's eye, otherwise he
would have at once brought it out before the admiring

gaze of what we will now suppose to be his fairly numerous patrons.

The direction in which this was located, however, seemed quite plain to him, and the road straight enough. There was no turning aside or retracing his steps in order to find fresh paths or commence the exploration of fresh regions in the hope of possibly higher attainments in respect of beautiful form; he had chosen one course, which he confidently expected would eventually bring to view the long-sought-for realization of his hopes.

This was on the line of simplicity. Doubtless he had seen going on all around sufficiently numerous and similar efforts made by contemporaries and deceased masters in his line, but without being disheartened.

We have no records of any peculiar system or the manner in which the many masters of the art of Cremona and other violin centres were trained; it seems scarcely possible that the highest standard of excellence among the liutaros there was reached by the casual admission into their ranks of youths who happened eventually to exhibit great talent or genuis for the branch of the fine arts to which they had been introduced by their parents or guardians.

Two stories come to my mind of liutaros of assumed sufficient natural talent to dispense with any tuition—self-taught men in fact, but their works give sufficiently strong hints that they were trained in the usual way, and displayed in their early works, one of them certainly, the characteristics of their master and the school to which he belonged. One of these instances is that of the first of the Gaglianos, Alessandro, of whom it had been related that having acted contrary to the laws of the place wherein he resided, he fled to a forest, where he amused himself with making violins.

Now the violin, simple as it is in structure and mechanism, is not to be made off-hand in a forest with any rough knife to hand; it poses as a work of art as well as a musical instrument, and must be carefully built in convenient premises with suitable appliances and tools. Further, the work of the first Gagliano speaks very forcibly of the maker having been properly trained in the atelier of Nicolas Amati.

With regard to the other instance, Giuseppe Odoardi, the fact of his being one out of three makers of the same name—and of these, probably the first in date was his father, all belonging to the same school—should alone be sufficient to cast grave doubts upon any probability of truth in the story.

That the numerous contemporary makers kept in touch with one another, at least, as regards style and workmanship, there is abundant evidence ; not only was their own work influenced by that put forward in their own locality by men of renown in the different working centres, but it seems to have been a custom for young practitioners to work for a time under the superintend-ence of some artist of established reputation, until such a period came round when they found themselves capable of getting along unaided, or had accumulated sufficient means wherewith to purchase necessary material ; this would include pine of such acoustical qualities as might be suitable for the class of players in the district where they proposed to work.

It was with proper and far seeing consideration of surrounding circumstances that Joseph Guarnerius, in the period comprising the years 1717 to 1720, or there-abouts, while making trial after trial of fresh patterns—none of them apparently coming up, in his discrimina-tion, to the standard of form and modelling which he had set out to discover and call his own—made a departure or distinct step in advance of what he had been doing since he had left his teacher.   Guided by his own artistic instincts, he was on the point of throwing overboard nearly all that had been instilled by that master of quaintness, Andreas Gisalberti.

What this departure was, with other details in connec-tion, will now have our attention.

It will be easy of perception that the prevailing idea of attempted gracefulness and simplicity is strong in both of the designs herewith illustrated. The waist curves, or C's as some prefer to call them, have all the qualities, peculiarities, or tendencies of a design that was to appear perfected some years later. It will be noticed that there is careful avoidance of the elaborately broken up curves, notwithstanding the elegance attached thereto, of the Amati. The straightness of the central portion, or tendency thereto, with the lesser top curve and bolder lower one as shown in the Stradivari design, is carefully avoided; possibly his own, to be called in the future by many of his admirers his grand pattern, was gradually becoming more distinct as time went on, and ambition was with no very faint hint holding forth hopes of his occupying a position some day, not much, if at all, below that of the then acknowledge heads of the craft.

The soundholes are getting more Cremonese—in the sense of the Amati and Stradivari school; Joseph was thinking more along the same line as regards their position and proportion; the form has lost most of the former quaintness, and only requires more study of delicacy at the extremities.

The modelling, although still belonging to the class or system termed "flat," has a slight rise inward from the channelling, reminding, in a very faint degree, of the old Brescian manner; but unlike Gasparo da Salo, it is continuous in character of form all round.

This peculiarity of modelling was much fancied by a late master of Cremona, Laurentius Storioni.

The varnish is of fine quality and transparency, and of a rich chestnut hue; the back is especially rich in figure. The pine of the upper table is close in thread. In length it is 14 inches, 8$\frac{1}{8}$ greatest width.

In the other specimen illustrated, owned by Mr. John Kirkhope, there is less of the peculiarity, as if the maker had become dissatisfied with it and dropped the idea.

It is, however, in other respects that the greatest changes have taken place, the first of which is in respect of the varnish. This, doubtless remembered in connection with the earlier violins referred to, had been subdued

MR. PETHERICK'S JOSEPH GUARNERIUS, 1718-20.

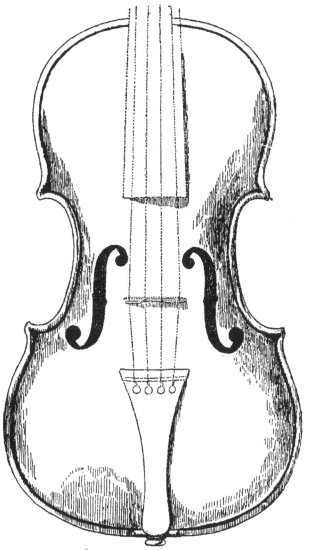

MR. KIRKHOPE'S JOSEPH GUARNERIUS, C. 1720-4.

yellow, orange and light brown, the latter particularly being thinly laid, soft in consistency, and somewhat frizzled.

In the earlier of the two specimens in hand there is noticeable a great leap in the direction of rich colour; apparently the maker had become alive to the advantage of more positive tints, or had received some urgent solicitations to clothe his work with a richer material— the colour is what may be termed a bright chestnut, appearing at times, under favourable light, to have a tinge of red. Full, transparent and beautiful, the use of such a varnish must at once have placed the maker in the ranks of the foremost men of Cremona's art.

On Mr. Kirkhope's violin the varnish has a deeper tinge and suggestiveness of what people called ruby red, also of the highest quality. In this instance also we can perceive an advance in the Cremonese manner of treating the soundholes, these being a still further depar- ture from his early manner, or Gisalberti period, the influence of the teacher being now absent, almost in the absolute sense of the word. The alteration of colour and consistency of the varnish was not the only altera- tion at this time.

Another one, which would seem but a trifling detail of construction when the violin has the upper table removed, is that of the linings or pieces running from one corner block to the other at the waist, mainly for the purpose of giving a broader glueing surface to the upper and lower edges of the ribs. They are now inserted on the system adopted by the Amati and Stradivari school, that is, instead of the lining coming to a full stop at the block, it is driven some little distance into it with a square end. The reasons for so doing are not very evident, excepting the holding of the parts together when the glue had become likely to give way under usage and age. The rough manner in which these linings were bent round, although the inserted ends were fairly well finished, seems to point to this part of Joseph's work having been thought of as a very secondary matter, and

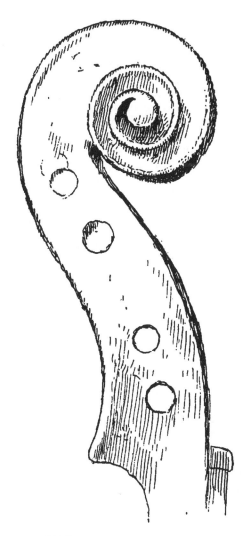

SIDE VIEW OF SCROLL OF
MR. KIRKHOPE'S JOSEPH GUARNERIUS.

not being seen from the outside, so long as they answered their purpose, were good enough. They are of pine, which being a wood rather disinclined to bending, has frequently snapped while being placed in position.

This fresh arrangement of the interior necessitated the placing of larger corner blocks so as to receive the linings, or so that the cutting of the grooves in which they were placed would not be likely to split them.

These linings are cut in such a manner that the threads may be seen, and even counted, if not obscured by grime, when looked for through the sound-holes. There can be no mistake as to the reason for so placing them, that is, with the threads not running ribbon-like flat with the ribs but at right angles with them ; this is to allow of bending with the least risk of breakage, but with all this precaution notwithstanding, such was the haste or impetuousness with which they were placed in position—possibly with insufficient heat while bending them, or, if wetted, not soaked through—that fractures are present in perhaps two or three linings of the same instrument.

The cutting of these to the desired thickness, that of about the same degree of stoutness as customary among other makers, is of a rough kind. The strips of pine being cut to a fairly equal measurement, were placed, or we might as well say forced, into position all round, after glueing in a rough-and-ready manner. These were—when set or dried, of course—chiselled round to make a thinner or bevelled edge toward the middle of the rib, the chiselling commencing in each case from the block.

There is nothing unusual or peculiar in this treatment, a little more strength perhaps and stretch of surfaces, or the attachment by glue of the upper and lower tables to the ribs being more firm.

Of the ribs or sides a word or two : they are not very thick in substance, rather under than over the average amount as left by a large number of the Italian liutaros of the time. As a most probable reason for this we may fix upon the fact of Joseph's wood being usually of rich

figure and more likely to break when under the strain
required for bending them into shape. That Joseph bent
them to the requisite curve by pressing them over a
heated bar of iron is evidenced by the fact of scorched
places being seen occasionally; here again Joseph
leaves traces of his tendency to hasten over parts of the
work that were of secondary importance as regards the
building up for general effect.

Further details concerning this not unimportant part
of the instrument may be of interest. That Joseph built
upon a block may be accepted as a fact; there is too
much in favour of it and nothing against it. The use of
an outside mould or block—the ribs being fitted inside
round the hollow space cut out to pattern—appears to me
quite opposed to the tendencies of Joseph in the whole
course of his work from beginning to end. It would be
consistent with the working of such men as the Amatis,
Ruggeris, Stainer or Stradivari, although it seems to me
very doubtful if they used it any time. The report that
any of them did so comes from a French source; it is
strictly in keeping with the ideas of workmen who never
manifested much originality if they really possessed it.
To a maker very desirous that all duplicate parts of his
work should be perfectly equal, the system would readily
lend itself as possibly the best way of getting exactness
of relationship of the parts.

The Italian liutaros as a class did not look upon the
matter in this light; the most finished workmen among
them, after the consideration of the tone given out by the
materials, bore in mind the certainty that the instruments
which left their hands would not undergo any examination of their interior except under such circumstances as
accident might necessitate, and when in the hands of the
repairer.

The good work was therefore on the outside, and
properly so, being accordingly made as attractive as their
skill and materials permitted; in short, they were artists
first and workmen afterwards.

Their imitators in other countries were firstly workmen, frequently of great ability, often having more mechanical exactitude about them than the men whose deeds they were emulating; secondly, as artists, but to this appellation, with the requisite talent of originality, they could raise no just claim. It was on the lines of the first that Joseph Guarnerius had from the first constructed his violins—fair work, such as was expected or even demanded as a necessity, characterised all his efforts, but of finely, delicately-finished or polished up interiors, he was not at all in favour; robust treatment with a sufficiency of refinement, character with elegance whenever possible, form expressive of masculine majesty rather than effeminacy, large sweeping curves rather than pretty subdivided ones, brilliant even gorgeous colour of varnish—these were the qualities that his genius had suggested for his ultimate aims.

They, however, were not to be obtained right off at once upon the mere inception; the curves, proportion, modelling, and consistency of the varnish had all to be carefully thought out before being put into practical condition; step by step each had to be grasped in detail and pressed into the service of the whole. Masterpieces of art are not executed at the outset of a man's career; this is not confined to one branch of art—in those of painting, sculpture, literature, and the more closely-allied one of musical composition, the grandest and most perfect specimens were not the first or even early attempts, but the results of long-continued persistent efforts at reaching an ideal, perhaps with some feelings of uncertainty of having attained to all that was possible. It will be still in the memory of some readers how Antonio Stradivari advanced by small, almost imperceptible changes in what might appear on first thoughts as matters of petty detail, until the more significant parts of his design gradually developed that mature structure of his late middle career, and beyond which there seemed to him nothing worthy of attainment. At the time this fully-completed idea was sent forth into the world as the climax of the judgment and experience of an artist who had been pronounced to have overtopped all the efforts of his predecessors on the same lines, there was Joseph Guarnerius—a much younger man, in the same city—steadily improving in his artistic skill, and about to win for himself an imperishable record on the roll of fame.

The question will doubtless have occurred to many, whether, in the absence of any records handed down to us directly, there was the probability of much, or any knowledge of each other between the two, or of personal acquaintance. There appears to be a plain answer to the first that there was; to the second, there was in all probability little or none.

The onward progress of both from the first had been a gradual development from the primitive efforts put forth after leaving their teachers.

In the one instance, Antonio Stradivari, on setting forth as an independent artist, by degrees threw overboard, as useless and cumbersome, that which he had been taught to look upon as a necessary part and parcel of his equipage on his voyage through life.

Precisely the same course was adopted by Joseph Guarnerius with regard to the teaching of his master, Andreas Gisalberti, later known at Santa Ballarini.

There was as much strong individuality and desire for advancement in one as the other, although they were working along in different channels.

The one had already attained to the summit of his aspirations, acknowledged as holding the highest position in the practice of his art; more perhaps was not possible to him, nor could a rival in respect of aggregate qualities have appeared in the least probable.

The other worked on in confidence and with enthusiasm, feeling that there was yet something to be done on one of the two lines which, however distinctly separate, were yet parallel.

It was thus as regards the position of the established master and the coming one; the latter, we may say, was (in all likelihood) at the time well patronized, as things went in those days. Joseph Guarnerius was able to lay

by a large stock of such materials as seemed suitable to
his views and intentions; this would not be effected
without the expenditure of money, perhaps much of it,
as the sycamore used by him at all times is mostly of the
richest figure; seldom, if ever, is it otherwise from first
to last. This, I think, will not be found in connection
with the career of any other master, all at times having
given out some indication of having used up their store
of fine figured wood and had recourse to that of inferior
or less pronounced figure, if in all other respects it was
as good.

The period now engaging our attention was one of
great importance when viewed retrospectively, and marking the commencement of another stage in the career of
the coming great artist.

It has been pointed out that about this time—that of
the introduction of linings on the Amati system—there
was noticeable the use of varnish more highly charged
with colour.

In the single transparency there was not much to be
done; it was in the consistency, number of coats, and
for all that we know there may have been some fresh or
delicate manipulation and refinement of the raw materials
before application to the surface of the wood. This,
without question, was for the purpose of enhancing the
general effect of the work.

The use of the somewhat cold, grey sycamore, that has
not turned brown with age, although lower in tone, of
identically the same quality as that of his teacher, and at
the same time, seems to point to their relationship in art
being sustained, and to their purchase of material from
the same market or district.

All artists of experience will recognize the fact that
when a cool grey body colour is glazed over—in reality
varnished—by a thin coat of highly-coloured transparent
material, the result of rich ripeness is not to be equalled
by any other means.

There is some analogy to this in the method adopted
for special brilliancy so remarkable in parts of the best

examples by Titiano, Tintoretto, Giorgione, Paolo Veronese, and other lords of the Venetian school of colouring, whereby a richness was obtained beyond which the world has not yet gone a single step.

That the two Joseph Guarneris took the hint—if not originally taught by some one—from some masterpieces of Venetian effect in painting, is not impossible; the effect having been noticed by a man of artistic instincts would be made note of, and put to a practical purpose in his own line of art.

Although the effects obtained by this method on many of the violins of Joseph Guarnerius were so striking, it was not his invariable rule to use the almost colourless undercoat, or priming, over his richly figured sycamore; at times the first coating was a degree warmer, or more approaching an orange tint, than at others. This may · have been almost accidental, or done with some amount of indifference as to the precise heightening of the colour. Acting on the "spur of the moment," or the humour occasioned by the surrounding circumstances, seems to have been so often the accompaniment of Joseph's work as to almost appear as his regular habit. The part of his career now under consideration would—without doubt—show further and stronger evidence of this, if at any time a few more specimens came to light; that many are still existing and likely to come under inspection at any moment, has been rendered probable over and over again by instances of other makers of the time.

CHAPTER XII.

Probable Reasons for the small pegs Inserted on
the Back and Front by Different Liutaros—
Further Modification of the *ff*—The Angles
of the Ribs—Manner of Securing the Neck—
Different Touches over the Scroll—The
House of Guarneri, Andrea Guarneri, and his
sons Joseph and Peter—Peter Guarnerius of
Venice—Relationship of the two Josephs—
Their Working Together—The Border—
Further Remarks on the Gouging of Scrolls
by Joseph I.H.S.

THERE is no particular date which can be, with
any degree of certainty, or even great probability,
pointed to as the moment of Joseph's departure
from what we may call his early middle period into that
in which there is scarcely a trace of the influence of his
teacher, Gisalberti.

That it was a rather rapid transition, and not a very
slow development, we may reasonably conclude from the
several, if not many, different changes in the treatment
of minor details during the progress of construction.

Our attention is firstly drawn to the absence in his
earliest work of the peg at each end of the back. The
makers whose habit it was to insert these pegs appear to
have mostly, if not always, inserted them in the front as
well, but in this position they are not easily discerned,
many having been cut through or withdrawn by repairers,
and the holes filled up.

From all that can be learnt upon examination of a very large number of Italian instruments, including the three sizes, as to the purpose of this peg, it was inserted for holding each table in position while some finishing touches were put, especially round the edges. That many makers of eminence did not use this little peg for steadying matters during the progression of the work, is neither for or against the appropriateness or advantage of its use.

Gisalberti does not seem to have been favourably disposed towards its use—that is on the back. Repairers and dealers have, however, in some instances, noticed its absence, and knowing full well that their great law-giver, Stradivari, was in the habit of inserting two in the position, have with most dutiful intention supplied the deficiency.

The insertion of the peg by Joseph seems to have become a regular habit from this time, as in his later works in good preservation it is with few exceptions seen. It may be remarked, however, that different from what might have been expected of a maker of such bold individuality, it is not large, but under the average size of those inserted by other makers, and so managed as regards colour and neatness of its setting as not to draw attention.

The next is the manner of affixing the side linings, already noticed in detail; the use of varnish of deeper or stronger hue than was hitherto his custom and that of his teacher, and the manipulating or affixing it in such manner as would enhance the general effect.

Further, the variation or uncertainty in the modelling with its many subtle curves; much care is taken to avoid more than a very moderate rise; in fact, during the whole of his career Joseph Guarnerius was not inclined to any sort of full modelling. If his fancy was occasionally for a slightly deeper channelling, with more emphatic rise inwardly, the central elevation was low, and coming quite within the term, as generally understood, of the flat model.

The designs of the soundholes begin to show signs of some influence external to what was going on around.

In the very early period they were upright, with a full-
ness of the lower portion, and with such character as
might have struck critics of the time—of which there
were probably as many as at the present day, that is
proportionately, probably a plentiful supply always at
hand—as being of a different caste to the usual
Cremonese school, with its clear indications of Amati
origin, and in which there was some substratum of truth.

Coupled with the inclinations of the upper part toward
the central line of the table, there is perceptible a desire
for better proportion; the lower wings are very slightly
hollowed. In this particular Joseph was strict in his
habit, so much so, that it is very doubtful whether he
ever cut any soundholes with an emphatic hollowing;
when it is present, close scrutiny may be rewarded by
the discovery that the work has been under revision
by some modern would-be improver having the idea of
making it more complete.

Yet another detail in which some alteration is made,
although but a trifle in itself, may be noticed, that of the
junction of the ribs at the corners as seen outside, which
is less sharp and more in the manner of the work done
by the liutaros of the place.

It has been noted previously that Gisalberti's fancy
was for a comparatively sharp angle at this part, in the
manner of Lorenzo Guadagnini, and other makers of
lesser renown.

In none of Joseph Guarnerius's work, after this period,
is this treatment followed out. His desire to work in
this particular on a different system was shown soon
after leaving his teacher.

At no time does this part appear to have been finely
finished or squared off with mechanical neatness. Just
enough of this for general effect was what he seems to
have been pleased to act up to as a rule. The middle
rib, after being fixed in position, has each end, on the
inner side, shaved off, continuing the external hollow of
the corner block to the extreme corner, or point. The
full thickness of the lower and upper ribs is retained all

along, and when pressed into position—the length being sufficient to allow of some projection beyond the middle rib—it is afterwards pared down; this makes, if well done, an invisible junction. There was nothing new in this, it being the common practice of the Amati school generally.

His old manner of securing the neck to the body of the violin does not appear to have been altered. All those that have come under my notice in sufficiently original condition have been treated in the same way, thus, the upper ribs have been made of one piece continuous all round, and before closing up the violin finally, a flat headed nail has been driven through the block into the lower portion, or root of the neck.

During this period there is no special or radical change in the treatment of the scroll; boldness is a quality present from first to last. Notwithstanding the fact of the influence of Gisalberti being present for the whole of the first half of the working career of Joseph, there is the stamp of individuality of thought and desire for progress.

The first turn, or the ear as it is termed, at all times invariably commences high up, and is well and openly gouged. The backs down to the shell differ, some being broader than others, all being somewhat roughly hewn out, and the majority shallow. The width is slightly greater as the lower part is reached; this is so with the scroll of Mr. Kirkhope's Joseph Guarnerius, illustrated on pages 115, 116, and 117.

The foregoing alterations, modifications, or improvements, as they may appear to the student of Joseph's work, although, perhaps, not the thought of a day or week, seem to indicate that there was some outside influence, and that they were not from intuition or the outcome of individual thought and effort at improvement.

There is no reason apparent to us why Joseph Guarnerius, after leaving Gisalberti's studio for one of his own, should not have continued—as large numbers of other liutaros did before and after him—to work on the same lines as his former master, with contentment and as much ease as circumstances allowed.

Assuming there is good ground for the supposition of outside influence, we will look around for a possible, or consistent, source.

We have no knowledge whatever of the exact spot in Cremona where the young liutaro, Joseph Guarnerius, first commenced business as a master. It is within the limits of possibility that when Gisalberti left Cremona for Parma—he was working at Parma in 1716—his young pupil and follower may have continued the business with the same style of work on the premises vacated by his master.

If this was really the case, he may have continued working industriously at many designs which are lost to us through the accidents of usage and other causes.

The position of "the house of Guarneri," which it may be assumed was that of "the great Joseph," is well known to people of the present day; it formed a portion of the block of houses in which were included those of the Stradivaris, Bergonzis, Ruggieris and the Amatis. It was nearly at the corner, and in a line with the first two. Joseph Guarnerius was therefore, in the latter half of his working career, in the heart of the centre of violin making at Cremona, and which had by that time been established for over a century.

I think it will be readily granted that there is very little likelihood of the young Joseph opening new premises and commencing business at such a spot at once after leaving Gisalberti. This would have been a very bold proceeding, such as could only be equalled by a young man of the present day, immediately after the termination of his apprenticeship in some outer portion of London, starting on his own account within a door or two of one of the largest and oldest established firms in the heart of the city. If we concede that there may be some possibility of the sort at present for a novice with plenty of capital at his back, there was still less in the times we are talking of. On the other hand, if we suppose the liutaro, Joseph Guarnerius, to have been working for many years up to 1720-30, he may have industriously accumulated capital enough to enable him to take a place alongside the dignitaries of his craft, and be in closer touch with the kind of patronage he was enjoying and ambitious of extending.

Falling in with this is another hypothesis concerning his working at this spot.

In putting this forward it must be at once granted that the ground on which it is built is not of great extent, nor plentifully besprinkled with facts that only require properly arranging; there are really very few.

The paucity may be accounted for by the want of knowledge or the consciousness among the liutaros of the neighbourhood that their works would be so much sought for, and fabulous sums of money paid for them more than a century after they were gone, and, in the majority of instances, they themselves forgotten where they had been for so many years busily making—as it afterwards proved—principally for future generations. If the hypothetical ground taken up is not very resourceful in its complement of hard facts, it may be said on the other side that there is little or nothing that can be urged against it.

We will turn aside for a moment, therefore, and look over what facts come down to us in connection with some of the other members of the family of Guarnerius.

The first of the famous name handed down to us as a violin maker is Andreas Guarnerius, who, tradition has it, was a pupil of the best of the Amatis, Nicholas.

As his work has every indication coinciding with the peculiarities and excellences of that talented family, this can be passed by without a challenge.

He seems to have been an artist with very little desire for striking originality. To him for a long time the Amati outline and modelling, or, as he may have considered it, the family style, was all that could be desired, and there did not appear to him any pressing necessity for radically altering the contour or changing the pro-

K

portions.   He was, however, Italian to the backbone,
and while putting into his work for some time all he
knew and had been trained to carry out, he could not
help throwing in a few touches of his own, if, apparently,
only to prevent people thinking of him as a servile
copyist of his famous teacher.   Now and then these
slight displays of individualism were enlarged upon by
him, causing them to be more conspicuous, and serving,
to some extent, as landmarks for the connoisseurs of the
future.

Briefly, his principal departures from the exact lines
of the Amati system consisted in an enlargement or
lengthening of the waist curves, sometimes to a considerable extent, and in giving a larger arching to the
upper part of the soundholes ; this causes the lower
portion to appear by contrast smaller and more turned
up.   They are drawn with unsurpassable neatness, the
cutting, or knife work, being equal in all respects to
that of the Amatis.

Not so, however, the other portions of the work.
Andreas Guarnerius was not happy in the cutting of his
sycamore; while working the softer pine he was content,
but when contesting with the tougher material used for
the head, sides and back, impatience showed itself, causing unsteadiness of line in drawing, and a suspicion of
uncertainty in the inlaying of the purfling.

Of his tone, it might almost be said as a matter of
course that it is of excellent quality, occasionally—
indeed generally—reaching a high level ; but, as with
the artistic part of his work, or that which appealed to
the mind through the eye, it was not of a kind that would
lift the maker above his fellows in the vicinity, which
was then the greatest centre of violin making the world
has known.

That he was duly versed in the mysteries of the finest
varnish of Cremona there is no contention : but he was
content with using a low-toned golden colour, or a soft,
rich golden-brown on most, if not all, of his instruments.

Andreas Guarnerius, although taking rank among "the

immortals" of his art, does not in any one respect take a place side by side with the highest.

His tickets seem to have always the sign of the house of business, and run thus, in the usual latinized fashion of the period :—

Andreas Guarnerius Cremonæ sub

titulo Sanctiæ Teresiæ 16 . .

This seems to have been the only kind of ticket he used. I have not seen or heard of any other being quoted.

He had two sons, each of them, like the second and third Amatis, far more gifted than their father in their perception of good general effect, and a long way ahead of him in originality of treatment.

The elder of these, born 1655, after being instructed by and working with his father, went to Mantua, with which place his name is associated by modern connoisseurs as a great luminary in the art of making violins, and he may also have been in his own day recognised as such.

His younger brother, born in 1666, stayed at Cremona, carrying on his work in the same premises as his father, that is if we can go by the sign of the house as quoted on his tickets, which are worded similarly to those of his father, thus :

Joseph Guarnerius filius Andræ fecit

Cremonæ sub titulo S. Teresiæ 16 . .

We may gather from this that on the death of his father, which, it is said, occurred about 1698, he kept the business going, thenceforward under his own name—how long does not seem to be precisely known. We therefore can only make a rough estimate, and in doing so, will refer to the well-known dates of his son, taught by his elder brother, Peter, in Mantua. The nephew, Peter

K2

Guarnerius, appears to have been well established at the time, 1725—1730, in Venice, a veritable hot-house full of many of " the flower of the profession," and to have become one of the leading names there, and recognised as having much more than ordinary ability and knowledge. Coupled with this was the necessary experience, not to be acquired within a few months. He possibly was doing very well there financially.

The date of the decease of his father (Joseph) does not appear to be known with certainty, it being put down at different periods from 1730—1739. He appears to have made violas and violoncellos, with occasionally other varieties of stringed instruments, but as to double-basses it seems doubtful.

There is something worth noting with regard to the end of Joseph filius Andræ, that is, that neither Peter of Mantua nor his pupil Peter of Venice, son of Joseph filius, came back to continue the business. There was in all probability some good patronage in connexion with the old established firm, and a question arises out of it as to whether the making of stringed instruments was stopped altogether in consequence.

It is here that the hypothesis seems reasonably to come in, that the premises were taken over and the business continued by Joseph Guarnerius, afterwards known as he of the I.H.S., and cousin—if the quotations are correct of some tickets said to be worded " Joseph Antonius Guarnerius Andræ nepos "—of Joseph filius Andræ, who was by about seventeen years the senior of the two.

With regard to the exact relationship there is some obscurity still hovering around ; there is the assertion that the whole name as above quoted has been seen on a ticket or tickets, somewhat in opposition to the fact that all those—recognised up to the present as genuine—in his well known instruments have only the two names.

The hypothesis may be further developed by taking into consideration the character of the work of the two Josephs at and before the period above alluded to.

The renown of Joseph Guarnerius filius Andræ has been in a great measure owing to the splendid varnish with which he enveloped his works. Without going to that extreme in praise of him which has been so often seen in print, that he was " the king of the varnishers," it may be fairly conceded that when his typical varnish is found on some of his more handsomely wooded instruments—his wood was frequently somewhat plain or wanting in what is known as rich figure—it seems to be endowed with such a rich lustre and hue that it may be thought not only unsurpassable but unique.

There was a particular variety which he was more disposed to use than any other, and by which his work is easily discriminated by connoisseurs, having a gorgeousness united to a perfect transparency and elastic quality. It may be described—perhaps as well as such a material can be—as a " salmon red " with a golden basis. Being evenly laid also, its presence is enough to enrich almost any figureless sycamore and draw attention away from any number of peculiarities of detail that may be drawbacks in the eye of the searching connoisseur.

If we allow the probability of junction in business matters between the two Josephs—cousins or what not—the explanation of the reciprocity of influence is not difficult to understand. On the one side we have the older and experienced artist relying principally for his general effect upon his wonderful varnish—his distinguishing characteristic in fact ; on the other hand, the younger and less experienced, but more highly endowed with natural ability, to be soon acknowledged as the manifestation of genius in freedom and masterful originality of design, at a time and place where progress or novelty may have been thought well nigh impossible or even unnecessary.

Thus, if we can imagine the connoisseur to have been present, the actual after circumstances or the result might easily have been foreseen,—the effort of the elder Joseph to infuse more piquancy of style into his works of art, and the younger clothing his with the aristocratic vesture suitable to the fresh surroundings.

That the later productions of "Joseph Guarnerius filius Andræ" were very strongly tinged with the style of his so-called cousin, has been widely and for a long time acknowledged. In view of the before mentioned probabilities this is easily explained. His want of strength as an originator—that is in comparison with the giant power of the other—who, we will now assume, had been working for some time with him—was, perhaps, still more marked when he strove, for his own advantage, to ingraft some of the salient points of style that he thought would help to make a telling design.

The verdict of connoisseurs has been that his object was not accomplished with great success; he was not endowed by nature with the requisite power of draughtsmanship, or he would, in the world's estimate, have proved a most formidable rival to his cousin.

It may never be known for what length of time the two were working together; it was, however, sufficient for the mutual influence to be felt, fixed, and transmitted to the works sent out by each.

I do not remember the name of any maker recorded as a pupil of "Joseph filius." If there was not one, then our hypothesis is helped further, although indirectly, and we may rest upon the supposition that when the time came that Joseph the elder was to lay down his tools, there was to remain the younger and stronger man of worth, thereafter known by his latinized name of Joseph Guarnerius, I.H.S.

Although up to the present it has not been possible to get in touch with instruments that are doubtless in existence, made during the period just referred to, and which would be of much service in our treatise, those at our command are very useful as illustrative of the manner and almost regular progression of Joseph Guarnerius towards what we may term the most popular period in his work.

The illustrations of Mr. F. Garrett's Joseph Guarnerius (*See Plates XXVI., XXVII., XXVIII., XXIX., and XXX.*) will prove very interesting in addition to Mr. Kirkhope's already referred to. The violin here depicted is specially interesting in having so much about it declaratory of the artistic efforts toward a unique or settled masterpiece of design. It shows that although Joseph had to all intents and purposes thrown over his teacher's ideas of effect, he could not help giving a look back and keeping a touch here and there, as if scarcely knowing it had not been originated by himself.

We still see something left of the extended swing at the lower part of the soundholes, which would not inaptly be termed an idealisation of his early or Gisalberti style, with the rather wide lower wing. There is the somewhat stiff run down from the top curve of the shoulder to the upper corner, and which now and again appeared in later times to the end, to the value of which in economy of the design, the master—for we must now credit him as such—was fully alive.

We have not yet the lengthened waist curves, or C's, as some like to call them, but there are the elements decidedly present of the large swinging line at the part that gave so grand a distinction a little later on—it may have been but one or two violins ahead ; one may mentally picture Joseph inwardly saying, "A little more here and there and I have got it!"

There is the modelling of low elevation, simple, as all great things are, and declining gradually to the edge with nothing to speak of in the way of channelling.

The corners have not been to any appreciable extent modified either in general aspect, or in the direction of the angle, nor have they more or less protrusion than hitherto. There is a steady adherence to a regular system. It was not as to these points that the master's alleged eccentricities were indulged in. If violins made during different periods of his career are placed side by side, the variations from each other will not be found so marked in this respect as some would be inclined to think. It is with regard to the lines leading to the four

corners, or angles, with the proportion of the parts, that
the master's activity of inventive power was chiefly
exercised. In the present instance there will be perceptible at a glance the intention of the designer, that
of extension in the curves at the waist.

For the accomplishment of this the lower portion
appears as if widened out, the consequence really of the
rotundity being less, or the curve being flattened.

The same remarks would apply, not inaptly, to a type
well known as a peculiar one of his cousin, Joseph filius,
but only to a limited extent, as the upper part of the
waist in that is, as described in some well known
criticisms, "hewn out under the shoulder," a figure of
speech good in sound without being founded on a
practical knowledge of construction of the violin.

The type referred to indicates that Joseph filius was
conscious of the imperfect proportion or want of balance
of the curves accruing from his development, but believ-
ing in the originality, or "taking" look of the design, he
set to work at correcting this by bringing the soundholes
lower down.

There was thus effected a counterbalancing of the
design, a means also adopted by Carlo Bergonzi, but
who, having greater skill in the management of contrast
and harmony of free lines, was able to bring about a
better result in the direction of what may be termed
artistical breadth of design, or freedom from pettiness.

There is over this design of Joseph, taken as a whole,
some remaining influence of his early working days,
when engaged in freeing himself entirely from tutorial
influence.

We may see this at the upper part especially, where
the curving is somewhat heavy, and suggestive of an
inclination to overbalance the lower, but the finely
conceived and entirely unmechanical waist curves come
as a full compensation for it.

The border is of fairly good width, with no special
emphasis at the central part, where so many makers
have thought fit to add effectiveness by a greater rise

above the purfling, causing the latter to appear em-
bedded. The purfling itself is of average neatness, just
enough to fulfil its part in the composition of the general
effect. The corners have the mitreing at the junction of
the ends somewhat obscured, as usual, and suggestive of
having been stamped with some favourite tool of the
master, but not equally so in all eight instances.

With regard to the head and scroll, of which Joseph
had early given indications of coming mastery in this
department of his art, there is displayed that boldness of
conception carried out with consummate mechanical
ability and ease in execution; there is no fine shaving of
line to get delicacy, all is the carving of a hand guided
by the mind that had conceived an idea and was working
it out in the wood.

The accompanying illustrations will be sufficient to
show the character manifested through the whole; here is
that fulness of line forming the front of the peg-box,
coming from underneath the scroll, that gives such an
assertive expression—a proud look, some would say, or
nobility.

There is fortunately the original neck with it, whereby
we can see the exact pitch or inclination of the head or
"throw" in relation to the run of the fingerboard that
was intended by the sculptor. Very often this is spoilt
by repairers, who, after sawing off the head for renewing
the worn-out neck, fix it again at an inclination suitable,
in their judgment, to the instrument, the result being in
many instances quite ludicrous.

The grooves running over the top of the head down to
the shell are rather wide, and of fair depth of gouging.
The shell itself is more fully developed than with earlier
specimens. It is at this part that Joseph from this time
—possibly a little earlier—showed more variation than
any other. Capricious with regard to the depth of
gouging, or even with the manner of modelling, it may be
said that after a run of perhaps some half dozen of one
type, he felt the need of a change, and the next specimen
would be not only a wide departure but a deeper one.

It may be suggested that the varying forms of this part may have been caused in later handiwork by the instigation of owners accustomed to the usual pattern of the Stradivarian or Amati school, but there would be little difficulty in detecting instances where this had been done, and the suspicion must be treated as in most cases unfounded.

In the accompanying photos of the head the focus of the lense has been a trifle too low, and the result is a slightly more oval form of the turns than in the reality.

The whole of the carving is exceedingly bold, and, as with all of his others, is done with great decision combined with freedom.

It is these qualities, combined with others that go to the making of a grand success, that have drawn the admiration of makers and connoisseurs of all countries since his time.

Signor Marchisio's violin is interesting from its having in repetition the same peculiarities as the foregoing one, the *f f* being low down and the modelling a trifle higher. The *f f* incline much toward the centre. The whole structure is of massive appearance, the back of finely figured sycamore in two parts, with the curls rising from the join upwards, and which was a frequent, perhaps favourite, way with him. The varnish is of a rich orange of splendid quality.

The character thrown into his work by Joseph Guarnerius, especially as regards the gouging of the scroll, must have been a matter of surprise to the critics and patrons of the time, if it did not even excite the "envy, hatred, malice and all uncharitableness" of some of his brethren of the craft.

Accustomed for so long a time to the delicate, effeminate, almost languishing beauty in the designs of the Amati family, and the development invested with a more regal air in those of Antonio Stradivari, their enthusiastic admirers found themselves awakened to the presence of genius in the branch of art to which it was directed. The works sent out by the artist from "the

SIGNOR MARCHISIO'S JOSEPH GUARNERIUS, C. 1725-30.
ORANGE COLOUR.

house of Joseph Guarneri " had such individuality and
force as to make people pause and think as they do
now when a " great Joseph " has been discerned by the
cultured eye as reposing amidst a mass of indifferent
surroundings.

Effeminacy of contour, meaningless lines, hard and
fast rules, adherence to antiquated forms and mannerisms
were now being studied as being of necessity things to
be avoided. Artistic proportion, masculine elegance,
forcible character, with free spontaneous style, were
placed before his patrons by Joseph ; in a word, thought
written legibly over the masterpieces to be fought for by
the connoisseurs and traders of coming centuries.

CHAPTER XIII.

STRADIVARI AND THE TWO JOSEPHS—JOSEPH I.H.S. AND
HIS CUSTOMERS—OLD ANTONIO AND THE CHURCH
OF S. DOMENICO—THE PROXIMITY OF CARLO
BERGONZI AND HIS TWO SONS—THE RUGGIERIS
AND OTHERS—THE INTERIOR OF JOSEPH'S HOUSE,
HIS WORKING APARTMENT—HIS STORE OF WOOD
—THE SIZES OF HIS VIOLINS.

IN THE comparatively modest premises opposite the
church of S. Domenico, a door or two from the
residence of the now aged patriarch Antonio Stradivari, our minds are led to the circumstances bearing
upon or surrounding the two men of genius exercising
their powers in an art separate from and independent of
all others, and which had been originated by a fellow
countryman about a century and a half before, and
which in a sense had become entirely native.

That Joseph Guarnerius and his cousin were to be
seen working together at the house, a reproduction from
a photograph of which forms the frontispiece of this book,
has recently been made something approaching a fact
from the information given me of two violins each
with a ticket stating the work to have been done by
Joseph Guarnerius in association with his cousin, Joseph
filius Andræ Guarnerius. The exact wording in Latin
on the tickets is not to hand yet, but if it turns out to be
satisfactory in all respects, it will transform the
hypothesis into the regions of dry fact, with additional
interest.

Our illustration represents the exterior of the house in which the cousins worked, in probably the condition and general aspect at the time when Joseph—the great —was occupier after the demise of his elder associate in art.

The bewigged connoisseurs and patrons were probably often seen, as depicted, leaving the artist, then of at least local renown, with perhaps his latest pattern of the time, his violins covered with the lustrous varnish of ruby or golden hue with which he had now almost become asso- .ciated among the dilettante of the place.

An occasional chat between Joseph and many of his clientèle would have proved interesting to us moderns had it been possible for some of them to be reported verbatim, on subjects frequently touched upon beyond the casual ones of daily remark—often, perhaps, concerning the pro- gress of his fame among musicians as a tone master as well as artistic constructor, reports also as to his free style in its rivalry with the old academic one of the Amati school; or of what was being done by the sons of the patriarchal Antonio Stradivari, themselves by now makers of long experience, one an innovator in some not unimportant details of the workmanship in violin making, an original designer too, although without the strength and resource of his neighbour.

The old Antonio, no doubt when standing at his door looking over at the church of S. Domenico, ofttimes cast a glance or two to the left, and may have seen Joseph Guarnerius, who was to be his acknowledged rival several decades later; and knowing his work, marvelled some- what at the almost impudent freedom of design in which the younger man of genius was indulging, perhaps influencing, or changing for the worse the public taste, or leading it—who could tell? Would it be to the down- fall of the Cremonese school? And then the patriarch, with a half audible religious exclamation, turns, with his long white locks fluttering in the passing breeze, to re- enter, with yet some nobility of bearing, such as was in harmony with that impressed on his violins years back, going slowly to his seat at the bench, doing just a little to an instrument that had been now and then taken up during a considerable time past, and which was by slow, very slow, degrees approaching completion.

We must not forget the close proximity of Carlo Berzoni, with his two sons, working together or at times separately, a man of almost equal talents with Stradivari or Guarnerius. His was a more fitful genius, at times pouring forth work worthy of the master with whom tradition says he worked; at others apparently obliged to seek the help of his two sons in finishing matters of careful detail. Living so near (only a door or two off) to old Antonio Stradivari and his sons, there is no unreasonableness in supposing him to have been often in and out of the Stradivari studio, helping in any of the different details, as he was versatile to an extreme.

Some of the Ruggieris were still working at their studio next to that of the Amatis in the Via Coltellai, the course of which was east to west, and might be said to be just round the corner on the right when the spectator stood before the studio of the Stradivaris or Guarnerius.

Other makers were doubtless busy close by in the neighbourhood, all having their own style and individuality, supported by their own following, some doing very well, and of whom we as yet know nothing to identify them with excellent work that turns up occasionally; others, whose names were well known in their day, have become, through the removal of their tickets by traders, quite lost.

The houses of Stradivari, Bergonzi and Guarnerius faced the church of S. Domenico, and looked due east. Those of the Amati and Ruggieri round the corner accordingly faced the north. From the difference in position chosen by the first occupiers in each instance, the north light, so much valued by artists in the changeable climate of Britain, was not considered a necessity.

The houses and the church opposite must have thrown a shadow of some hours' duration over the premises of the first three mentioned, and at other times the direct rays of the sun would not be so powerful as might be expected under other conditions.

During the period of which we are treating, the eminent liutaros referred to, with probably others of less note, scattered round about in the neighbourhood, might have been seen at most hours of the day, excepting at the heat of noon, active in the different departments of designing, carving, glueing, or varnishing works, which for centuries after were to be looked upon as masterpieces of a byegone age, and of an art lost or enveloped in an impenetrable mist.

An apparently ordinary wayfarer may have been seen passing along in front of the three houses of the liutaros facing the church of S. Domenico, bearing perhaps less than to-day any external signs of what was being done within ; he looks upward at the sign of the house, " Sancta Teresa," and he knows it is the one he was seeking. Entering with the polished mien of the upper classes of the period, he finds himself in a room of modest dimensions used for both work and business, evidence of both being on all sides.

It is here the final touches are given by the master's hand. There is the bench on the left side with a few gouges, chisels, planes, and small saws here and there, while on the walls round about are to be seen small metal patterns for working details.

A few violins are hung on the opposite wall, which to the eye of the intending purchaser are of the ordinary type or style of the maker he has been advised to seek. A small nest of drawers, with a bottle of ink, quill and pieces of paper, are near the window, a chair of the period for the occasional visitors to lounge in, massively carved in the manner of the day, with large curves, vulgar enough to suggest inappropriateness of lodgement near such refined work as the proprietor had placed in view. His own seat, used for hours at a time, is near, and of no pretensions. It is strong enough, with its leather padded top studded round the sides with brass-

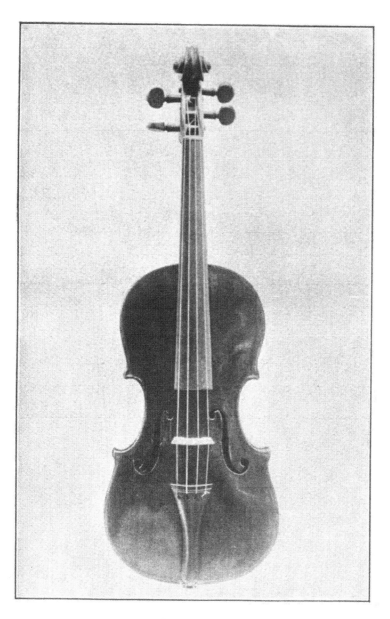

Plate XXVI.
VIOLIN, JOSEPH GUARNERIUS, C. 1720.
Owned by Mr. F. GARRETT.

Plate XXVII.
VIOLIN, JOSEPH GUARNERIUS, C. 1720.
Owned by Mr. F. GARRETT.

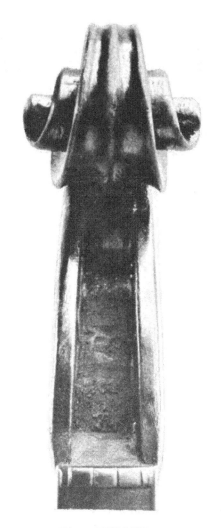

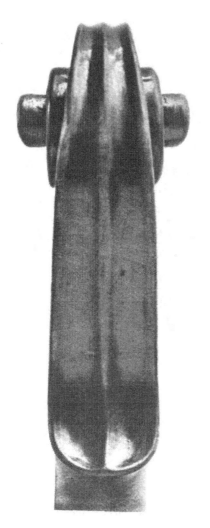

Plate XXIX.
VIOLIN, JOSEPH GUARNERIUS, C. 1720. SCROLL.
Owned by Mr. F. GARRETT.

headed nails, for his life-time, and maybe for two or three others after him.

There is a cupboard in one corner with its door ajar. Inside can be just discerned several bottles carefully fastened up and a label pasted round, but the light is not sufficient to enable one to read them several paces off, and possibly being private matters, they were not intended for perusal by ordinary eyes.

This apartment forms about one half of the ground plan of the premises, a door half open reveals the other, or back half, much more rough in general aspect than the front. The walls have nothing over them. Nails here and there have suspended on them the larger tools of various kinds for the earlier stages of rougher work, done now by one or two assistants, who are actively engaged in measuring and separating pine and sycamore to be ready for the master's attention by and bye. Through two windows a very small back yard can be discerned, in which some large, roughly hewn logs can be espied, perhaps recently brought in that state from some particular part of a forest known to the master and a friend or two.

The choice pine from some half dozen selected trees is kept indoors.

The pine is of a class and individual character selected by Joseph from time to time from a particular part of the country, perhaps known only to himself and his former teacher, Andreas Gisalberti. The latter was at this time working—when not engaged in other branches of art, and he is reputed to have been of skill as an architect—at Rimini, a town on the east coast, and about twenty miles north of Pesaro.

The cherished store from which the now renowned liutaro occasionally took a piece suitable for particular requirements, was in all probability carefully marked to facilitate the selection, and cylindrical portions of the tree itself, if of small circumference, cut into convenient lengths to be again divided into longitudinal sections.

A heap of such we may suppose lying in a corner, or

L

resting against the bare wall of this back room, having
nothing about it that would be attractive to a casual
observer; but to the master, who may have been
frequently seen turning them over, they had more than

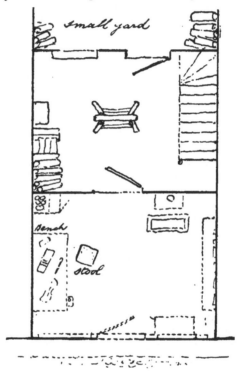

PLAN OF HOUSE OF GUARNERI, WITH
PROBABLE ARRANGEMENT WHEN
JOSEPH WAS WORKING THERE.

ordinary interest. It was from among these carefully
conserved portions of precious raw material that some of
his now most famous violins had their upper tables or
sound boards cut. There is a fairly large amount of that

famous cloud-marked pine still to be worked up, notwithstanding the liutaro having withdrawn pieces from time to time since the year 1714. There is enough to use, interspersed with other varieties of the same pine, at the liutaro's usual rate, for ten years or more to come.

That this was so is proved by the fact of this tree being recognised as having been used in the construction of some of the latest known violins of Joseph Guarnerius.

We have no facts which lead to the supposition that Joseph thought more highly of this particular tree than any other.

The grains, or threads, are on the average less regular —although fairly straight—than that observable with some of the other trees used. The cloud, smoke line, or stain, is not an unusual mark met with in the materials used by the old liutaros of Italy.

A similar one has been noticed on some of those of Hieronymus Amati, Giovanni Grancino, and others. These are not, however, accompanied by the peculiarities of grain, or signs of growth. To properly recognise the "Joseph stain or cloud," a study of the other special marks of individuality in conjunction is necessary. The distinctive mark is not always apparent, although we may be certain we are looking at the same wood. It may therefore have not extended along the whole length of the tree. Possibly, too, the mark did not accompany the progress of the few rings all round, and may have belonged to a part either most exposed, or least so, to the rays of the sun, or to the action of currents of air.

Storing of wood from particular and suitable trees appears to have been a custom among all the prominent liutaros of Italy; but although this is a generally accepted fact, we cannot gather much knowledge from it; there is still the question, how did they know that the particular tree would give the identical tone required? Other questions arise concerning the place, means and reasons for selection, and all of which are involved in mystery, perhaps never to be unravelled.

We have assumed that Joseph Guarnerius stored his

L2

valued pine in the room behind the front shop, as we
would now designate it.   There it would be conveniently
at hand on requirement, more so than upstairs, of which
there is, of course, some possibility of a further storage
of material.

It is possible the sycamore was kept more exposed to
currents of air, and probably in the open sort of attic so
common in Italy.   The comparatively hard and tough
wood of this particular growth favoured by Joseph,
necessarily required a greater length of time before
being thought safe to use, and under these circumstances it was likely to be attacked by that arch enemy
of the fiddle collector—"the worm"—and of which in
some of Joseph's violins there is unmistakeable evidence
of his cognizance when cutting the wood into slabs and
shaping it for the lower tables or the head, he having to
fill up the tunnellings with pieces of the same material.
We have in this evidence that the liutaro looked upon
the richly curled sycamore as too valuable to be lightly
put aside.

In the back room alluded to, Joseph would have
probably one or two assistants either helping, or doing
work in its preliminary stages as learners.   We have
supposed him to have been superintending some operations when the visitor or patron calls in, perhaps to
request that one of the violins that he has just noticed
be delivered into the hands of his servant when calling
next day, and for which the money is placed in Joseph's
hand, and the contract duly carried out.

The visitor departing, Joseph takes his seat and pro-
ceeds to work ; it is upon a violin of the proportions so
frequently seen, being a sixteenth or an eighth under
fourteen inches in length from edge to edge, exclusive of
the button at the upper end.

Although sending out so many of these dimensions,
there are occasionally met with others that are longer
than fourteen inches ; there are many more in proportion
that are shorter, but of full width, the most likely reason
for this being the varied requirements of the players of

the day, who were thus enabled to secure the quality of tone in request, with an instrument suitable to their handling.

In our day this is changed. Whatever the height or size of the performer, he must have a violin of what is thought to be a standard size, that is, as exactly as possible fourteen inches in length, no matter whether he be a burly giant, or a shrivelled dwarf. The same fashion rules with regard to the length of the bow, whether the player be tall or short.

CHAPTER XIV.

Joseph's Masterpieces in his Prime, when he was
in Possession of all Necessary Means for
their Production—His Teacher Still Alive
with a Nickname—Joseph Taking Hints from
the Works of Others—Mistakes about Joseph
Working with Stradivari: how Caused—The
Greatest of Scroll Carvers—Reference to
the Different ff of Joseph—Joseph Continuing the Business on the Decease of his
Cousin—Other Masters Altered to Pass as
Joseph's Work; Curious Frauds—Adaptations
of Details by Masters from other Works—
The Varied ff of G. P. Maggini.

WE have now arrived at a period in the career of
Joseph Guarnerius when some of his finest
productions were issued. Those modest premises in the same line as those of the patriarch of the
craft were to be the starting point whence issued masterpiece after masterpiece, for which masterpieces—those
which may have fortunately survived the ravages of
time and tinkers—money in daily increasing amounts is
demanded, keeping pace with that paid for the finest
examples of the work of Joseph's near neighbour, old
Antonio.

The reasons for the advance to the front by Joseph are
several, and like all men of genius who have made for
themselves a name famous and historical, his genius
was not one-sided. No man of first-rate renown

in the different branches of pictorial art, music and literature, has been distinguishable by one quality alone; it is invariably by the combination of several that eminence has been achieved. The great artists of the renaissance were not men who could do but one thing with the touch of genius; they were one and all more or less men of great power in other directions than the one in particular by which perhaps their light was especially magnificent, and whereby they overshadowed their contemporaries.

Thus the man of genius, Joseph Guarnerius, commencing his career on leaving his teacher, believed in and relied firstly on the special tone quality of his violins, using at the same time timber of the highest degree of excellence, such as appears to us now to have been beyond acquirement by the majority of his fellows in the craft.

Circumstances being eventually favourable, or necessitating his removal to the premises of Joseph filius Andræ, a great advance was made in the direction of rich colouring of the enveloping material, or varnish.

During the ensuing years up to 1735—being in possession of all the necessary means and skill in application for the production of works of very high merit, equal, in fact, to the demands of the musical community—Joseph's ambition was to be completely on a level with the greatest masters of the liutaro's art who had hitherto been known. His handiwork, when scrutinized, gives strong indication of his having studied many styles in succession. Andreas Gisalberti was still living, turning out his quaint, almost grotesque, patterns at Rimini. Gisalberti when at Parma used a printed ticket there, and working at Bozzolo for a short time in 1717, went to Rimini the same year. It was therefore, in all probability, at this place that the circumstances occurred under which the nickname of "Santa Ballarini" was given him, and which he adopted on his tickets.

By this time Joseph had thrown him aside as completely as was possible; scarcely anything remained that would bring back a remembrance of his first instructor in the craft, excepting that indenting at the mitreing of the purfling at the corners. There is, however, another detail still retained—the slight stiffening of the curve running down to the upper corners, which being an almost absolute necessity for contrast with other parts of his later designs, is kept but faintly so.

As related of great luminaries in other arts, Joseph, when looking round for hints and points of suggestiveness, did not hesitate to affix to his own patterns and modellings any little touch or modification which he fancied, and that appeared to him as likely to enhance the value of his own productions. That he studied the whole range is evidenced by the attachment to his work of small details peculiar to each that came under his observation.

Thus over one modelling may be noticed a tendency, very slight and of low elevation, to the ridge along the centre introduced by Nicolas Amati; when copied by other makers it was much exaggerated, and formed what has been called the " hog-backed " model.

Another was a little dip down, apparently left in the finishing stage of the point of the upper corner, very slight and only noticeable in well preserved specimens; the same being found at the lower corners. It was the outcome of an effort to give piquancy of style, and was one of the developments proceeding while influenced by the ideas of his neighbouring fellow craftsmen of eminence. The most marked change was in the treatment of the border. This part in the hands of Antonio Stradivari seemed to Joseph to be better than what had been done by himself up to the time when he entered his present premises. He accordingly took a hint or two concerning the width, elevation, and distance of the apex from the extreme edge.

Another hint from old Antonio was the position and proportion of the sound-holes, and the increased elegance arrived at. No direct copying, however, is to be seen, only the influence of a near neighbour and great master.

It may have been the management of these parts that led so many people to conclude that Joseph Guarnerius must have been a pupil of Antonio Stradivari, or worked much with him and his sons. This idea once getting into print, was soon accepted as more than probable, and afterwards copied, re-copied, and then treated as a generally accepted fact.

More than this, the enthusiasts, following up this line of reasoning, have pointed to some of the later scrolls of Antonio's violins as giving strong indication of the handiwork of Joseph—witness the emphatic touch of the gouge and the ear, and which they either could not or would not believe possible in the hands of the old maestro under ordinary circumstances.

These admirers of the two masters would have been wiser had they, while conducting their examinations, postponed their conclusions until after they had reviewed, in proper rotation, the work of each done at different times, and under various moods when working; they would doubtless have then arrived at the fact that the peculiarly dug out, or emphasized, ear of Joseph's scroll was not constant, but only occurred at intervals.

There are sufficient specimens still extant to enable us to review and compare the whole of those known as carved by him, and perhaps a good majority will be found free from this peculiarity of touch. This must not be understood to mean that the gouging of the rest is of the ordinary manner of other makers of his day; every scroll that he carved had some distinctive character thrown over it peculiar to the designer, and reaching a level of originality and excellence that may be said to have been his own.

Every part of the scroll seems to have been from time to time subject to whim or changeable humour. If it be said that as a rule the turns in a so-called typical specimen have a bold open swing, the next one coming to view will possibly have the first turn rather small, the " ear " being close to the axis, or " eye; " the other parts will, however, compensate for this by more than usual openness, or width. The back view, in a very large majority of instances, will have the first cut down rather suddenly; for a long time I thought this an invariable practice, till suddenly an unmistakeable specimen of the master's work came before me with the first turn as full in development as any types of the Stradivari school.

Another part of the head, the grooves running down to the shell, has been frequently referred to as typical of Joseph's handiwork. These, to appear as " the proper thing," ought to be shallow, roughly gouged, and the shell itself rather broad, and with a tendency toward square- ness in the manner of Gisalberti, of whose influence it may be called the remnant.

In this direction also Joseph was, for the connoisseur, as uncertain in his humour as with the other details that have been touched upon, as, after looking at some half- dozen with the shallow grooves, we come upon one with the reverse tendency, having a deeply hollowed shell, thus showing Joseph's rules to be no hard and fast ones. Another detail also was subject to much variation under the hands of Joseph, the contour of the part below the volute, and known to most as the peg-box.

The "throat," as the front portion of this is frequently called, varies considerably among different styles and types, some makers keeping steadfastly to one form, or as near as they could, others varying considerably.

This part and the corresponding back line admit of the finest perception and execution of flowing line. With some early makers the peg-box, back and front, was treated simply as a means to an end. We therefore find on a general average that it was without beauty, sometimes stiff, coarse and positively ugly. The Amatis, Ruggieris, and Stradivari, infused a quality of drawing into this part that must have been entirely unconceived of by other makers, notwithstanding the ability shown in other directions.

Refined and beautiful as the great masters had made this throat line, there was to the mind's eye of Joseph Guarnerius a possibility of endowing it with a different expression. Knowing that on the drawing of the lines of this seemingly inferior portion of the structure, the set, or pose of the scroll depended, he set to work and soon turned out those masterpieces of design that not only drew admiration from all connoisseurs, but eventually stamped him as the greatest of scroll carvers.

This is not to be thought of as a detail having exceptional attention and talent concentrated upon it; each part taken alone would not be of great artistic value; it is when viewed as a whole that the genius of the designer and executant shines out.

While throwing his energies into the development of these individual details, Joseph was no less careful concerning such parts as affected the mere user of the violin, perhaps as a tool simply, in the hands of some performers. The opening of the pegbox is of ample width. There is not the difficulty in getting at the string hole of the A peg as with the violins of many other masters. In this respect he kept pace with the best of the line.

The peg holes are also attended to, it may be said particularly so, as the D peg-hole comes rather close to the A, leaving good room for the fingers to ply between the pegs and the G and E, which are also close to each other.

With regard to the width downwards from the back of the scroll, Joseph seems to have concluded that the proportions adopted by old Stradivari were good, and left no opportunity for improvement.

The soundholes as here delineated have been traced from the different instruments, and are of the exact size. The first, letter *A*, is a typical soundhole of Andreas Gisalberti, having the characteristic details of form prevailing in a more or less degree in most which have come before me. Noticeable at a first glance is the pose or inclination, the upper part leaning back towards the border, thus being quite in opposition to the general custom of making the upper hole approach the centre line. The expression given to the soundhole is that of the upper hole trying to keep as far from the middle as possible.

The next, letter *B*, is that of Joseph Guarnerius, with the ticket dated 1706. This may have been his earliest one issued. The soundhole is interesting from its close

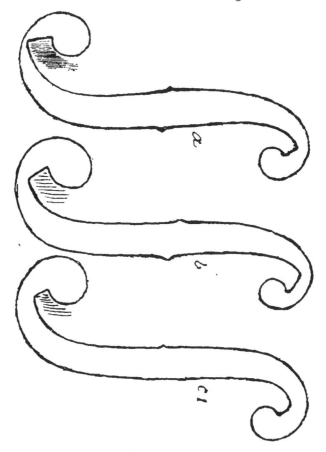

resemblance to that of his master, the chief point of difference being its more upright posing. The largeness of the lower part, with the wing fully developed, almost too much so, is at once striking.

Letter *C* is interesting from the evident effort at independence and improvement. The cutting is cleaner,
the posing is still vertical, but the lower portion and wing

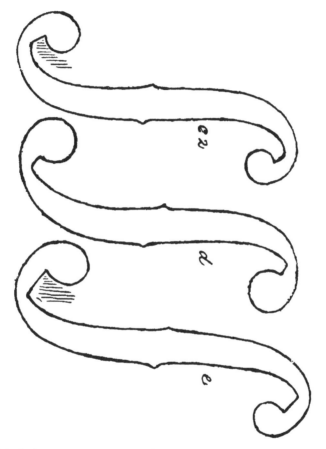

(this being narrower and further away from the lowest
curve) are lighter.

The next, *C*2, belongs to a smaller violin ; it is of the
same type with but little modification in detail. There

is only a little more bend in the upper and lower curves.
Letter *D* shows a striking departure, in almost all
respects, from the style hitherto favoured by him; so

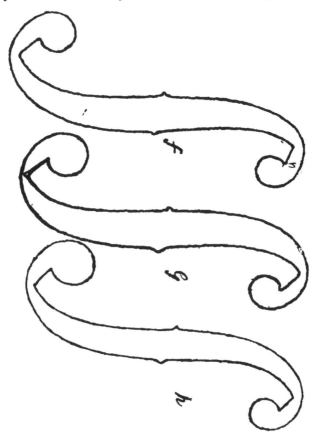

different is it that but for the rest of the instrument
declaring itself unmistakeably the work of Joseph Guarnerius, the design of this soundhole would scarcely have
been recognisable as his. The upper hole is enlarged,

both upper and lower wings are narrow, and the whole shorter than any preceding type. This may have been an exceptional design to suit some purpose ; however, the

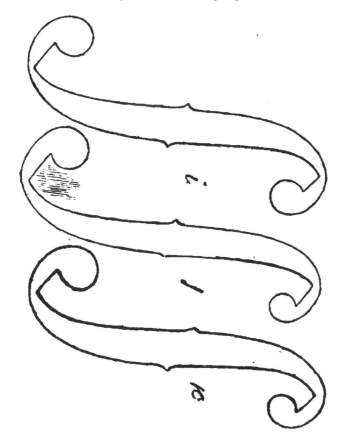

following one shows a resumption of his older kind of progress, and we here see some promise of what is to come in the better, or more Cremonese proportion and style, these doubtless being from the influence of surroundings, and in all probability when he had settled down with his cousin in partnership.

The accompanying tracings of soundholes from different specimens of Joseph Guarnerius's work are interesting, as showing the progression or variation in form. It will be observed how the later ones—*i*, *j*, and *k*—are lengthened, being amongst his most finished, and cut with a decision, combined with delicacy, impossible to excel; *k* is the forerunner of the more freely drawn ones, among which are some of striking individuality and even curious design.

It was to this part particularly that the connoisseurs of times gone by were probably directing their attention when they concluded that Joseph Guarnerius must have been taught by Antonio Stradivari.

In one sense this may be regarded as a reasonable supposition. Joseph, having without doubt well examined the works of the acknowledged master of the time and place was, notwithstanding his strong native disposition to keep to a style of his own selection, and let nothing divert his aims, ever ready to snatch at a hint that might be of use or that could be advantageously grafted on to his own design.

The alteration or improvement in his treatment of this detail was of the most simple kind, and effected easily during the progress of the work—in fact it might appear to many as an inconsiderable trifle, but judged by its results it was a masterly touch. There is nothing apparent on first observation beyond a careful attention to avoid a rapid tapering of the back upwards from the shell. The width is kept almost equal as far as the level across where the D peghole is situated; above that it lessens in the usual way to the narrowest part at the top.

A comparison between the works thus treated by Joseph Guarnerius, Antonio Stradivari, and most of the independent makers of the time, will be followed by a decision in favour of the two masters; more mature, classic in proportion, greater stability, will be the verdict.

That this was no mere thought of a moment, to be

Plate XXXI.
VIOLIN, JOSEPH GUARNERIUS, C. 1735.
Owned by Mr. H. HAVEMEYER, U.S.A.

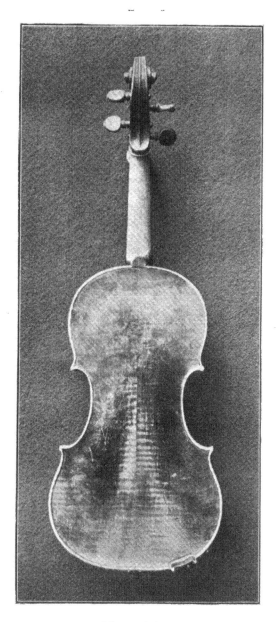

Plate XXXII.
VIOLIN, JOSEPH GUARNERIUS, C. 1735.
Owned by Mr. H. HAVEMEYER, U.S.A.

Plate XXXIII.
VIOLIN, JOSEPH GUARNERIUS, C. 1730.
Owned by Mr. F. P. FRANKLEN-EVANS.

Plate XXXIV.
VIOLIN, JOSEPH GUARNERIUS, C. 1730.
Owned by Mr. F. P. FRANKLEN-EVANS.

Plate XXXIV.
VIOLIN, JOSEPH GUARNERIUS, C. 1730.
Owned by Mr. F. P. FRANKLEN-EVANS.

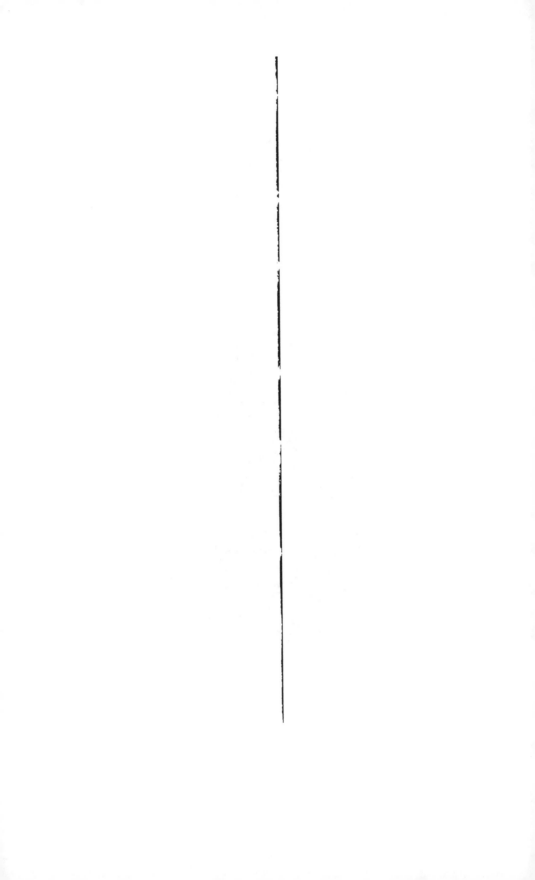

lightly dismissed, is confirmed by the attention paid to it during the remainder of Joseph's career.

After the decease of his cousin or partner, known to the connoisseur as Joseph Guarnerius filius Andræ, there is much likelihood of the patronage enjoyed by that artist falling on Joseph, our subject, almost as a matter of course. It is a misfortune, however, that between the years 1725 and 1735 so much of his work is lost, or has not been brought to the notice of connoisseurs. That much of it still exists there is no doubt, and many works, some of them possibly masterpieces, may at any moment suddenly emerge from their obscurity to delight the connoisseur, collector, and concert performer for many a day.

There are the same difficulties surrounding their rediscovery or restoration to the broad light of modern appreciation as there have been with regard to the earlier works of the great artist, and indeed for a long time even to the actual existence of his master. In a great measure they arise from a disinclination on the part of many people to move out of a narrow and confined path, and for the sake of comfort and as much freedom from anxiety as possible, they recognise only such specimens of work as may be compatible with their idea of a particular class, or period, in the artist's career which is known to them.

Thus to some, far too many it might be said, there is only one pattern for a Stradivari, that of his so-called "grand period," the others, really forming the large majority of his works, are "might be's," "probably's," or copies by a pupil, or even by himself, of his master, these latter being mostly known to them as "fiddles with long corners."

Further, through this recognition of but one general type of a master, his genuine work has often suffered by being mixed up with that of his pupils, or other makers, in a style somewhat similar.

Thus the work of Paolo Maggini is as often as not mixed up with, or asserted to be that of his master,

M

Gasparo da Salo, and he again frequently with individuals of the Pesaro School, "because it is rough enough."

If those who are desirous of really going into the study properly, with an idea of certain discernment of the works of different masters, would carefully study the habit of work, mannerisms in drawing out the designs, and also the direction of effort to achieve results in the instance of each master they are brought in contact with, they would find ample reward in the satisfaction of finding many masterpieces of the liutaro's art lying neglected or unknown, and might be the means of placing these in their right position, before the ever increasing numbers of those who are qualified for appreciating them.

It is from the lack of students trained in right methods of observation that so many masterly works have been lost, spoiled or ruined, divided up, the parts distributed abroad to be joined to parts by other makers, taken apart again, rejoined after "a lucky find" to other parts by the same maker, but not of the same instrument.

Improvements are occasionally tried; the work in its original state being thought lacking the special or spicy touches of the master, the owner or repairer, sometimes both, trying to implant some of the supposed interesting points associated with a late and better known period on to an early work, with a somewhat confusing result. Thus I have known a middle period Joseph Guarnerius to be touched up so as to pass as a late one; this no doubt was a happy thought at the time, and the executant felt that it was "sure to make it go."

A fine specimen of Joseph's more finished and delicate designs (*See Plates XXXI. and XXXII.*), belongs to the longer waisted or "large inner bouts " type.   The border is not broad, and the purfling is of neat insertion; the whole work has over it an air of great refinement and artistic excellence, the curves being a masterpiece of Italian drawing.   The corners are not very much indented, and the points at the mitreing are more accurately adjusted than on the average.

In the rise of the modelling or vaulting it may be classed as belonging to the usual low or flat type.

The pine of the upper table has the "cloud or stain" running down each half for the whole distance.

This head, as usual, has some signs of apparent haste, the outer "cheeks" of the pegbox showing some of the file marks that had not been quite obliterated by the glass paper finishing. Another interesting detail for remark is the fact of the A peghole having been pierced too high up at first, and another one made below. There is the stroke of a knife under the upper peghole seen underneath the varnish. Curiously the first one was left open and not filled up before I saw it.

The holes may have been intrusted to the care of an assistant, and when the master overlooked the work he drew his knife across underneath. The scroll had been "black edged" like so many violins by Stradivari, Bergonzi and others. The varnish is of a splendid orange color and of exquisite quality and transparency, giving, over the back especially, a gorgeous aspect.

The tone is clear, large and refined.

In length it is of the usual about the period 1735, a trifle under 14 inches with about $8\frac{1}{8}$ greatest width.

The sycamore is of the usual fine quality, the curls are a trifle narrower than the majority, and run at right angles with the join in the middle.

The $f\,f$ deserve notice, they being more Stradlike than usual, and moreover cut with a decision and accurary never excelled by any master.

Other makers have been requisitioned to supply the want of more Josephs; old masterpieces in their line from Venice having fine varnish, have been thought good subjects to work upon; Gobetti, Montagnana, and others, whose coats were thought red and rich enough, have been, after the treatment necessary for the purpose, passed off as Joseph Guarnerius, I.H.S. In their eagerness to obtain the amount of money the master is believed to command, third or fourth rate instruments have been transformed to deceive those who have not made themselves sufficiently acquainted with Joseph's work of hand to be on their guard.

Perhaps in this direction it would be difficult to find a more ingenious fraud than that accomplished many years back by a fiddle trickster who, obtaining an Albani violin with "pickled cabbage coloured" varnish, found the modelling too high for his purpose. Whether the tone was also of the "pickled cabbage" sourness is not related, but I was told that the difficulty concerning the high model was overcome by separating the upper and lower tables, damping and subjecting them to pressure until they assumed sufficient flatness to impose on the intended victims ; when put together again on the ribs, these were again shifted a little to accommodate them to the fresh conditions, and the whole was thought perfect. Frauds of this kind, it may be observed, are almost entirely in connection with the works sent out by Joseph Guarnerius during the period now under consideration— 1735 and afterwards.

Why this is so requires very little thinking over. The public have been long accustomed to having one or two particular types presented by dealers for their admiration, or the copyists have directed their attention to some specially handsome specimens. Those knowing anything of Joseph's work before that date number but very few, and are only to be met with among the painstaking connoisseurs, or earnest students of the subject ; indeed, so little is known of his work before this time, that an enquirer among the " dealers in Cremona violins " for a specimen of Joseph Guarnerius's work before the date referred to, or before 1730, would meet with very little satisfactory response, assuming him to be the possessor of a modicum of knowledge.

Up to this time, as we have been noting, Joseph appears to have been making efforts, earnest and continuous, at reaching the ideal of his imagination, this doubtless for a long time being in a hazy or nebulous condition. This was to ripen, centralize, and be the declaration of the genius within him, besides showing the help obtained from constant observation of what had been accomplished by men of acknowledged high standing in his own or other cities.

That he was capable of being influenced—we need not go so far as to say led—by the smartness of some designs that had now and again attracted his attention, there is much evidence.

This must not be taken as detracting in any way from the quality of originality; the latter is a term often misconstrued in its bearings with regard to the branch of art with which we have to deal, as it is likewise in the sister art to which it was to be so admirably suitable a helpmeet.

Originality in a design, as a whole, is quite consistent with the presence of component details which have served other purposes before.

In pictorial art it can be asserted without fear of contradiction, that the greatest masters of all times have not been able to present a grouping, or posing, such as was perfectly independent of anything that had been done before. In architecture it has been likewise a development; in musical composition also the grouping of notes in succession has been a gradual modification and adaptation of forms that have been previously used with different intentions, and less knowledge of their possible improvement in combination.

Thus, with regard to the present point under our consideration, there is perhaps no minute detail in the design or handiwork of either the master whose work is now under analysis, or the one whose lustrous star of reputation he was about to rival, which had not been done in some way, or been, in a manner, hinted at, before.

Taking the middle bouts, C's, or waist curves, as a sort of keynote of the whole design, the typical one of Stradivari in his so-called grand or golden period may be not unfrequently seen, in embryo some would say, among much earlier types, even of the Brescian school.

Both Gasparo da Salo and Paolo Maggini put forth a

violin occasionally that would seem to require very little modification in order to appear as a veritable design of the Cremonese master of more than a hundred years later. So with other Brescian makers, besides the first two masters—they had been put forward as having anticipated the typical Joseph Guarnerius pattern many generations before.

It may be freely conceded that if the waist curve of Stradivari's pattern consisted simply of the straightening or flattening of the middle portion, and that of Joseph Guarnerius of the lengthening of it, and shelving out of the lower part, then there is but little originality in either of the two typical designs. The manner of shaping this part would not alone be sufficient to impart the desired character, which could only be obtained by the harmony or contrast of the rest of the curving in other parts.

This may easily be tested by taking a tracing of the waist curves of any violin and fitting to them different upper and lower portions; the variety of expression given by the inequalities or balancing of the curved lines, the flow or opposition, will prove instructive to those who can take pleasure in watching the apparent changes in character of form under different circumstances.

It is in the artistic perceptions that the majority of the old Italian liutaros have so greatly exceeded the skill of those foreign to the country, and the latter doubtless have done no little brain-racking in their efforts to compete with artists who were seemingly "to the manner born."

To resume our course. Joseph Guarnerius, improving in the knowledge of the guiding principles connected with the practice of his art, was watchful that their application should be helped by sufficiently dexterous handiwork. He was about to prove his competency to rival on occasion the oft-praised mechanical precision of the greatest masters of Cremona. That it was not his everyday habit to work in one groove, trying to impress the connoisseur with the remarkable steadiness of his hand, we have more than sufficient evidence.

His natural bent—and the one which he was most pleased to follow out—was towards the display of character of form, proportion, and generally rich effect.

With a store of handsome sycamore, pine of the finest acoustical quality—such as he had fixed upon in early life as the desideratum of the future—there was no reason why he should not, at the fitting opportunity, put his powers of neat workmanship into force.

That the opportunity did occur now and then has long been well known, but the meaning has been misconstrued. The believers, in days gone by, of the tutorship of Joseph Guarnerius by Antonio Stradivari, thought the occasional insertion of the purfling with exceeding neatness was the outcome of careful training under the great Cremonese master, whereas the opposite will now be seen to be more in agreement with the actual fact of his tuition under Andreas Gisalberti *alias* Sante Ballarini.

Having watched his progress as well as all details of knowledge concerning Joseph Guarnerius will permit, we may assume, with a good show of reason, that he was in receipt of good patronage, and that his position in the craft was acknowledge to be high.

His own personal qualities as an artist of great talent were being openly manifested. His ripened thought, executive ability, and wonderful perception of the constituent items necessary for the production of magnificent results, were added to rather than thwarted by his preference for a more free style of treatment than had hitherto been attempted.

Many instruments had been made during and before his time that might be by some considered free in treatment, inasmuch as the results were the outcome of carelessness, and therefore, in fact, not good. With Joseph Guarnerius the conditions were reversed—the freedom of style was acquired after long practice, much thought, and possibly much experiment.

It was in the designing of the soundholes that he lavished so much of his great power of line drawing, which was coupled with the sharpest, cleanest knife work. So much was this so that upon a great number of his admirers this portion of the work leaves its greatest impression.

The "Joseph soundhole" is a term with no less meaning in it than that of the "Stradivari soundhole," with perhaps the exception that the former covers a much wider ground, the variety of expression given to this interesting part of the structure by the younger of the two masters being such as to attract at once the eye of the connoisseur, who then wishes to see others, as many as possible. The more seen the more wanted. No other master was so prolific in the output of his soundhole variations, excepting it may be Giov. Paolo Maggini.

This master, it has often been more than hinted, was the one, who more than any other, held some mysterious influence over Joseph. There is no room for doubt that the latter was not slow to perceive the advantage of some of the salient points in the late designs of the great Brescian, but that there is anything at all Brescian in the work of Joseph, probably no connoisseur would admit. As before stated, he, like all other great initiators in art, was eager to snatch at, and affix to his own design, anything that appeared to him worthy of annexation and absorption.

The same hypothesis would apply to his formerly supposed tutor Stradivari, whose soundholes were, at the period of which we are treating, called into requisition and made to do duty so far as fit.

In some of Joseph's "carefully executed" instruments, as some references are quoted, the soundholes may be termed a modification of the Stradivari type of his best times, but having introduced into them more spruceness or piquancy of treatment.

This has been effected at no cost of elegance of shape or proportion; it might even be without fear of a charge of heresy asserted that the difference is in favour of the younger master.

Passing along we find variations of this same type.

The total measurement in length and breadth is much

the same as with the Stradivari; but a touch here and there along the course from the upper to the lower end imparts an expression of more life; it is, in fact, the manifestation of the artist's mind in the direction of ease and freedom of line, as opposed to the mechanical confined style adopted by so many of his contemporaries and predecessors.

Combined with this was a wider lower wing, but not in the least like a return to the somewhat coarse and exaggerated one of his earliest working days, and many of the kind cut by his master.

All along there is perceptibly an aversion to anything like a depressed curving at either end of the soundholes. With the more Stradivarian tendencies in some they were accompanied by a slightly sharper arching of the upper curve above the angle of the wing; the latter also is in accompanying it more acute.

This tendency towards the "gothic" style, as some termed it, was retained by Joseph with variations, according to the humour of the moment, to the end. It was evident to him that a low curve, or less rise in the upper and lower curves of the soundholes would not bring what he wanted—vigorous expression. The drawing and knife work are very delicate in execution; the whole not so pleasing perhaps to the admirers of heroic types, nevertheless bearing the stamp of greatest artistic excellence.

Although from their style they seem to foreshadow the more lengthened-out ones of the period of 1740 to the end, they are not actually longer than the average, or of Stradivari's.

With regard to the contour generally of the violins of this period, 1730—1738, there is a distinction of style that may be said to belong solely to Joseph Guarnerius.

The modelling is of low gentle rise from the purfling to the middle, with the smallest possible channelling. In this particular he appears to have gone a step further than Stradivari, who is supposed to have given to the Cremonese school for the first time the so-called flat model, a title that conveys but a vague notion of the actual form.

To understand the term properly, many specimens of different modellings, but all taking the same length of soundpost, may well be studied; the intricate, although not very positive curved surfaces of many violins being of a misleading character, and often conveying a false impression.

The near approach to the border of the most emphatic part of the convexity will cause an appearance of much greater rise in the modelling than is really the case. On the other hand, a very slow rise to the apex of the curving in the centre of the upper table will give a much flatter appearance.

It was to more of this last kind that Joseph mostly, perhaps entirely, gave his attention. In earlier times he had, although keeping within the bounds of what might still be considered a low modelling, occasionally given way to a whim for having a fulness just a little on the inner side of the channelling, but probably feeling dissatisfied with the results, he dropped the idea.

There is the double advantage of this very slow rise from the purfling—that of the lasting power of the instrument under usage and repairing. There is greater power of resistance to strain in the low model in consequence of the fibres of the wood, particularly the pine, being longer and not cut through. With a marked channelling, the repairer, we will say of the average type, is necessarily hampered by having to guard against cutting quite into the channel while overlapping, and so having double work.

There is, too, less liability to the swelled appearance at the upper and lower portions of the front table through the prolonged pressure of the bridge, not to mention the pressure of the lid of the modern case, which too frequently has had little or no attention paid to its suitableness for its occupant.

CHAPTER XV.

THE LOW MODELLING OF JOSEPH NOT ENTIRELY HIS
INTRODUCTION—THE LONG WAISTED JOSEPHS—
THE PERIOD 1730-40—FRANCESCO STRADIVARI—
THE NOW EXPLODED STORY OF JOSEPH'S IDLE
LIFE, ETC.—CARLO BERGONZI'S IMITATION OF THE
STYLE OF JOSEPH'S HASTY WORK—THE MAKERS
WHOSE WORK HAS PASSED AS "PRISON JOSEPHS"
—EFFORTS AT THE TIME TO OBTAIN JOSEPH'S
TONE QUALITY—JOSEPH'S VARIATIONS IN DESIGN
AND EXECUTION—FURTHER REMARKS ON JOSEPH'S
SCROLL VARIATIONS—THE TREATMENT OF THE
RIBS BY HIM—HIS USE OF SALICE FOR LININGS
—SOME PARTICULARS OF WELL-PRESERVED IN-
STRUMENTS—JOSEPH'S BAR, HIS FINGERBOARDS
AND TAILPIECES.

JOSEPH GUARNERIUS has been sometimes
credited with having introduced the very low rise
of the modelling, or, as the more popular term is,
the "flat pattern."

It certainly was not his introduction, some very low
modellings having been used by Gasparo da Salo more
than one hundred years before, and he was followed in
this respect by his pupil, Giovanni Paolo Maggini,
besides others of the Brescian School. The Cremonese
must have been for long so familiar with the positive
rise of the modelling of the Amatis, that the lower and
more extended curved surface of Joseph's violins may
have seemed to them as an original and striking idea.

Be that as it may, the facts of the introduction of the low model by the inventor of the violin, and its resumption and retention a century and a half later, prove conclusively that it was no mere haphazard speculation, but careful calculation of requirements for making what had appeared an impossibility—an advance.

This lowering of the arching was accompanied by an almost entire absence of the channelling. There was sufficient left for artistic effect, however, the master (as by this time he must have been acknowledged to be) never losing sight of this.

During this period, which some would call his best, many of his violins have enough of what is termed "finish" about them to satisfy the most fastidious and exacting critic.

Prominent among the varieties of the same type sent out by the same master were those with a longer waist curve; they have been described as having "the grand long inner bout," which term, although good, does not give sufficient indications of the kind of design.

The inner bout, C, middle loop, or waist curve, whichever we may call it, is not expressed in the best manner by that term, as it is not the length that constitutes the difference between this line of Joseph and that of other makers. Many may be met with having an apparently long waist, but without the artistic excellence, and certainly with no suggestion of grandeur.

The line along its course merely is not of great extent as compared with others. The first in date of the Guarneris, Andræ, placed at the same part a wonderfully long one; Della Costa did likewise, Hieronymus filius Nicholas Amati, besides others of less ability or renown, tried a large loop. Joseph's efforts seem to be towards that which, while striking the ordinary observer as the acme of simplicity, should be of the utmost tenderness, the very opposite to a geometrical one, and not a fraction of which could be drawn by rule or compass.

Minutely analysed it will be found by no means so

simple in its proportions as the first glance would lead us to suppose. The small parts have no exact repetition, and the greatest projection or emphasis is placed with soundest judgment at the part most likely to aid in the general effect. Had it been a little below or above, the whole design would have been altered, and not for the better.

It was the less accurate perception in the selection of position for the apex of the curve that caused many otherwise excellent designs by the contemporary liutaros of Italy to take a secondary position, and be less attractive in the eyes of the general public.

It must not be supposed that in directing great attention and extraordinary skill to the management of this part of the design, Joseph neglected other portions or treated them as secondary in importance ; the opposite was in fact the case. If the many slight variations of the general type of this second half of his career be carefully considered, it will be seen that as the changes of the one part took place, the others had to keep company, and be harmonized accordingly.

The years 1730 to 1740 (*See Plates XXXIII., XXXIV., and XXXV.*), must have seen Joseph busy with his now fairly settled general type of violin—the outcome of many years of thoughtful consideration.

That such consummate ability in the adjustment of line in its relation to beauty of proportion, as demonstrated by the upper class of the famous liutaros of Italy, was mere cleverness in the execution of a few neat lines, amounts to a simple impossibility. The fact of their varying their patterns while adhering to the style that was congenial to their individual fancies, points distinctly to mental powers of which their successors and imitators appear to be destitute.

Joseph having now a settled style—his own, and which had made him a maker of mark and distinction—was doubtless favoured with ample patronage, which enabled him to secure materials of the highest class, apparently selected from the best sources, as no instances seem to be known of his using any but hand-somely-figured sycamore, and this of the best texture and density.

With regard to both form and colour, he must have now held a position inferior to none.   The veteran Antonio Stradivari, a door or two off, was taking a posi-tion as among past masters—his patriarchal age pre-cluding the possibility of fresh invention or disposition towards novel departures in his art.

Joseph, now well and permanently established, was sufficiently strong to influence his contemporaries—in a word, he was copied.

So soon as a position is attained by talent in art, then the certain acknowledgment comes in the person of the copyist.   Imitators of the style some may with justice be termed, and these do no harm to the originator or to the surrounding devotees of the art.   Sometimes, however, mischief results.

Genius often causes rivalry where it might be least expected.   We have seen that old Antonio's age was not favourable to the exhibition of jealousy, but there were other and younger men of somewhat the same age as Joseph who were affected by his prominence among the liutaros.

Take the nearest, Francesco Stradivari, the son of Antonio, and whose work at the present day is not so well known as it might be with intelligent search by connoisseurs.   He left many violins at his decease, mostly very fine, some masterpieces, others with strong indications that he was a thinker.

He had the misfortune (as it might be termed) to dwell under the shadow of his father's reputation, where-by his own excellencies appeared, by comparison, less evident.

In all probability the "spreading" quality of the Joseph Guarnerius aroused within him the spirit of emulation, and he, by the brilliancy of many of his violins, showed his desire to be on a level with the then head of a school of liutaros in Cremona.

There was, however, another maker, master-minded and but little, if at all, below any in native talent, who has left behind some indications, so far as his work could do, of jealousy or envious feelings towards the brilliant Joseph Guarnerius. This artist was Carlo Bergonzi. A man of extraordinary attainments in his art, who could at will turn his hand in the direction of the highest finish or the most sketchy off-hand kind of work.

He was also a very gifted designer, with great originality, of almost a daring kind, but of which he appears to have been insufficiently conscious, or which was not appreciated to the extent of his desires.

From the frequency with which his soundholes are placed low down, in this respect having probably the same reason for so doing as Joseph filius Andræ, it may have been that he had a particular class of patrons, these being possibly identical with both makers. Herein there is no difficulty in perceiving some hint of a foundation for jealous rivalry between the neighbours, Joseph Guarnerius and Carlo Bergonzi.

There does not appear to have been any indication left as to the source of knowledge or training of the latter, apart from the tradition and suggestiveness of his style; we are therefore left to draw any reasonable conclusions that may appear to fit all or most of the requirements of the case.

As to whether he really worked at any time with Joseph filius Andræ we have no positive evidence; both were among the greatest varnishers of Cremona, the colour and consistency of the splendid material with which they enveloped their works being frequently identical.

The tone of each, however, when critically analysed and compared, is more favourable to the hypothesis of Carlo Bergonzi having been Stradivari's pupil, and of his having worked with the sons of Stradivari, Francesco and Omobono.

Placing this aside as argument, we have the fact of the aged patriarch Antonio and his two sons working next door to Carlo Bergonzi, whether in a kind of partnership, or simply helping during pressure of business, we know not, but there is the greatest probability of very close intimacy.

We have here the accompanying and surrounding circumstances appearing favourable to a hypothesis of jealous rivalry on the side of the trio of the two Stradivaris and Bergonzi.

This, if accepted as in a degree probable, will be found in harmony and agreeing with the bearings of a story circulated in the early part of last century concerning the working career of Joseph Guarnerius. This has been well commented upon in Mr. Fleming's book on the violin. This story was said in the first place to have been delivered to the public in 1838 by a grandson of Carlo Bergonzi, a relationship that may not have been too far apart for the jealous feeling to have descended, and the concocted story, like a dirty snowball, having grown as it rolled; but under the open sky and sunlight it has now melted and become a thing of the past. The story was that Joseph Guarnerius, idle and dissolute, after some years of incarceration, died in prison in 1745. This was deemed a suitable little fiction for fastening on to the reputation of an artist who had grown so famous, and the lustre of whose reputation was obscuring by comparison the renown of the best known member of the Bergonzi family. The part of the story as to which there is most need for examination is that referring to the violins supposed to have been sent out to the world by the said Joseph Guarnerius while in prison. Apart from the improbability of an idle man becoming industrious while in prison, that place is not one in which we could expect violins of a high class to be made, however well disposed the prisoner might be during the time referred to—about 1745.

The story having been well implanted in the public mind, to agree with it and help it in every way, fiddles had to be found of a kind that might suit the fable. The more hasty works of several makers were brought into requisition, among them those of Laurentius Storioni of Cremona, Joseph Dall Aglio of Mantua, and Carlo Bergonzi of Cremona.

The latter turned out some instruments that probably seemed exactly suitable to the believers in the idea of such a thing as a "prison Joseph." One of the most versatile of all the host of Italian liutaros—Carlo Bergonzi—could and did in turn execute work of the most opposite kind and degree of finish ; so much so, that at one moment he may be known to take the place, in an important public sale, of Antonio Stradivari, and to be sold at a proportionately high figure, at another passing as the before referred to rough "prison Joseph."

Carlo Bergonzi's violins appear to have been first introduced to the British public under the name of Joseph Guarnerius, the tickets having been duly removed before arrival, consequently very few with tickets have their original ones. It is, however, with those of a particular class, or as they may be designated, departures from his original and distinctive style, that we are concerned at the present moment.

From the many details about them being so suggestive of the maker's knowledge of his near and successful neighbour, there is the greatest probability that they were sent forth, not as identical copies, but as violins made in a similarly free style to those of Joseph Guarnerius, and thus obtained a proportionate share of patronage as a result.

The general appearance of these violins is such that at first sight they are suggestive of the work of Joseph. It is when the details are closely examined that the real authorship becomes evident, and then we see that there is no actual imitation with intent to deceive. There is the approach to ruggedness of outline so frequent with Joseph. The corners are indented, the purfling broken here and there as if inserted in great haste, and the soundholes are what connoisseurs would call "Josephy"; the modelling too is very similar.

Further, there is splendid varnish of the highest class, laid on lavishly and apparently with a careless hand.

N

There is sometimes a seeming attempt at repeating the waist curve of Joseph, but if intended as such (and I doubt it) there is failure, the purity or simplicity of proportion and the grace being absent.

As a final piece of evidence, the quality of the tone is not Joseph's, however excellent it may be thought by critical ears. It is as if the maker, taking his soundboards from the same wood or district as Stradivari, had picked out some which he thought would be especially brilliant in tone results, and possibly more penetrating than the tone of Joseph; if so, there was again a failure, as the penetrative power is obtained at the cost of some mellowness.

There is some evidence that Francesco Stradivari was also anxious to put forth a tone of fine brilliancy, emulating in this respect the efforts of Carlo Bergonzi.

If this is true, it will be a good indication of the impression among the liutaros of Cremona concerning Joseph's powers, otherwise there would be no inducement to alter the course of the Stradivarian lines on which they, with others, had been working so long and so patiently.

As before observed, Stradivari the elder, being of great age, was very likely past being interested in the progress of events in which his two sons, with the clever Carlo Bergonzi, were more immediately concerned; occupying an important position, and with long experience, they could be left to themselves. A noted amateur and collector of the time is said to have remarked that there were even then signs of decadence in the art of the liutaro which had so long maintained its prestige in Cremona.

This was the assertion of an accomplished connoisseur who had dived into the subtleties of the art, and knew the stumbling-blocks that were the cause that would lead to the final collapse in Italy.

We left Joseph Guarnerius in the full high tide of prosperity, with ripened powers in design and execution. These terms, used in connection with almost any other liutaro of the time, would have necessarily been used with some reserve; with Joseph they mean power in wonderful fecundity of fresh ideas and new combinations of form, while sustaining the high standard achieved with regard to rich general appearance, and last, and not least, the glorious tone-quality sent forth by his violins.

These, if not sufficiently impressed upon the cognoscenti of his day, were to grow year after year in the estimation of the public, and the collective powers of the master were to receive full recognition.

At the time now under consideration, 1735 to 1742, Joseph may be said to have been achieving results hitherto unthought of by others in the branch of art.

In a corresponding period of other men's careers, which are so frequently lauded as their golden or grand period, there is one type, or it may be almost called one pattern, with very little variation, considered perhaps by themselves and their admirers as near the acme of perfection as it was in their power to reach.

With Joseph Guarnerius it was otherwise. He had, not the mere ability to turn out a violin of a type gradually matured after long and severe effort, but the power, with consciousness of it, to bring out fresh ideas of strange, almost fantastic expression over them, with an apparently inexhaustible store in the background to fall back upon for further developments.

His pattern in consequence was ever changing, the soundholes seldom twice alike, the purfling in substance varying as the other parts of the instruments, sometimes being a fair distance from the edge, giving a full width of border, these being mixed with others having a narrow border, said by some critics to be accompanied by meanness of general aspect, but which was very distinctly shown by Joseph to be not at all a necessary adjunct, as in these instances he has managed, notwithstanding the asserted risk, to impart an air of importance which commands respect.

There is also considerable variation in the rise of the modelling, this in some instances being what might be termed a common average, while in others the rise is

N2

very slight and gentle from the edge, the idea of channelling seemingly being almost laid aside.

One of the most celebrated violins by Joseph is very remarkable in respect of this detail, as at each end the channelling, although of very little depth and not below the level of the purfling, ceases gently at the waist, and the surface of the purfling at the middle is really higher than the border.

This arrangement would by some critics be attributed to Joseph's desire for the extension of the arch at this part, the channelling, as an accessory of inferior importance, having to give way to it.

There seems to me more probability of its being but a momentary passing idea.

In carving scrolls Joseph was as irregular in his fancy as in the designing of the soundholes, the disposition of the time or even moment suggested the particular expression of this head or capping of his work.

It is useless to search for the particular or exact cutting attached to any particular type; according to the humour of the moment so the gouging took place. Thus if the connoisseur expects a run of emphasized tooling at the first turn or ear, and with the frequent decline in the line downwards, he will in a moment be disillusioned as to its being a habit, as the next one of the period will have little or nothing of the same manner.

Thus the view from behind of the turns or volutes of the Stradivaris shows the line of the first turn downwards from the axis to be almost upright as a hard and fast rule. Carlo Bergonzi has a still more rigid downward line, which gives that strong development of the ear, for which he, in his own typical and strongest character, is remarkable.

Joseph Guarnerius, during a long run of his varied proportions in the gouging, will give you an impression that he carefully abstained from this, and was content to treat this part in the manner of Gasparo da Salo, which was to lower this most fragile portion and lessen the liability to accidental fracture.

You expect him to continue on in the same manner, when suddenly he treats you to a surprise ; the first turn and a half are kept closer than you thought him capable of, and the line from the ear is as vertical as with Carlo Bergonzi. In other details of small cutting, Joseph is as capricious as in the foregoing.

By a very large majority of the Italian makers the centre of the axis measures to the different outside parts about the same with each instrument, as if the same guide lines for gouging had been for years in use.

With Joseph it is the other way ; two or three may be similarly treated with regard to this part, and then comes the surprise—the axis is high up, and perhaps in the next instance low down, further so than you have seen with any other master.

So with the shell at the back of the head ; a number of these will convey the impression that the very shallow gouging of this part was an unvarying practice with the master, but the deeply scooped shell of the one you take up afterwards will tell you differently, and that the artificer was only keeping to one line so long as his fancy prompted him.

Notwithstanding these divergences from a regular beaten path and returning thereto, there is a singleness of intention present all over the work, accompanied by decision of purpose. The principal and leading thought is masculine boldness, strong individuality, and expressiveness, suggestive, to the beholder, of determination.

Polished surface was of secondary importance; his most imposing scrolls have less of it than others, the work being doubtless left at the exact moment the required effect was obtained. The most finished specimens belong to the period 1734 to 1738.

There were certain lines or limits over which he may be said never to have stepped. The following are the principal ones—the upper end of the peg box underneath the scroll is ample and roomy; Carlo Bergonzi was occasionally the other way.

The first turn is, although fairly high up, never carried

quite to the top as by some makers, nor is it kept close to the axis as with Peter of Mantua. The edges, or walls, are substantial, rising high above the deep and emphatic cutting along the course to the widest part.

From the frequent and great difference constantly taking place in the general contour of the scrolls of Joseph Guarnerius, we might almost be led to think that they were cut out without reference to guide lines, just as a person might whittle a piece of wood. This is, however, not in unison with the fact that we meet with two or three of the same period and pattern with very slight variation between them.

The inference to be drawn from this is, that having made his measurements or guide lines on paper, or other suitable material, he worked from them, probably pricking the course of the turns in the same manner as the Amatis and others, although not, as they did, keeping to the same for a hundred times in succession, but making a change after the third or fourth one had been completed.

A few particulars concerning the interior and make in the more mechanical sense may be of interest.

As touched upon before, we find Joseph working on the same lines as his teacher, Andreas Gisalberti. The linings were of full depth, not let into the corner blocks ; these were both substantial, roughly hewn pieces of pine, probably the coarser parts being used up after the upper table had been sawn out, as customary apparently with many other liutaros of the time.

The sides or ribs, very seldom continuous round the lower part, were sawn from the same piece of sycamore as the back, not always of continuous or even thickness. This may have been from want of proper care in the use of the saw in cutting the slice of veneer, or to the completing process outside. The middle or waist was affixed on the block or mould first, the ends shaved down at an acute angle, and the upper and lower ribs fitted to them. The average thickness of the veneer forming this part is one-sixteenth of an inch bare. This is fairly general throughout his working career. They were worked down to this with a rather fine-toothed plane; there is some indication of the preliminary sawing being of a rough kind. There is not much seen of this work, contrary to what many people would expect who think Joseph was a rough workman. Carlo Bergonzi and many other liutaros left much more evidence of the toothed plane with a coarser gauge. The ribs were bent over a hot bar (the scorched places being sometimes seen), not by wetting as practised by many makers.

That the more frequent division of the lower ribs at the tailpin was not from carelessness or indisposition to the work, is proved by the fact that the upper ones were perhaps more often than not continuous.

They were glued to the upper blocks while the latter were on the mould. After being separated from the mould, the back having been as a matter of course glued on previously, the blocks, both upper and lower, as well as the side ones, were reduced.

In doing this, one or two specimens of Joseph's work in its original condition show that a gouge of about five-eighths of an inch in width was used. This was, very likely, one of Joseph's more frequently used tools for general work, the surface presenting after its use a series of hollows not at all like the even, highly glass-papered surface left by Stradivari.

The neck (in one piece with the head) was fitted outside, and a flat-headed nail driven in the centre of the block through the neck, after which the upper table was glued on in the usual way.

It is not possible to point to a precise date at which Joseph altered his arrangement of the middle rib linings from the manner of his master, to that usually practised by the makers of note in the immediate neighbourhood. We can only estimate a probable period, which would be when he had been working for some time in company with his namesake, and who may have thus far used his influence in inducing the very independent minded artist to conform to the usages of the class of liutaros by whom he was surrounded.

Having once adopted his manner, that of inserting the square ends of the middle linings into the blocks, he seems never to have departed from it.

They are kept mostly a little closer to the rib at the insertion in the block than was the custom with Stradivari, who was regular in his habit of making the lining describe an angle or shoot into the block away from the rib. This to Joseph seemed to be an unnecessary attention to a part that was not meant to be exposed to the gaze of any person beyond a possible repairer in the future, and of whom he took no prospective account. Another change in the same part was not effected till the last years of his life—this was in respect of the material used for the blocks and linings.

Following for so long a time the practice of his master in using pine for these details of construction, we are surprised by the presence of the wood known to some as sallow, willow, or salice, in the interior as used by Stradivari and others of his school.

There is nothing whatever that can give us a hint as to the reason why Joseph was, in his last days, suddenly it appears, animated with the desire to put blocks and linings of the same kind as did his neighbours.

If we argue that the ease of cutting and bending was a probable cause, we are met with the fact that Joseph does not appear to have singled out any pieces that seemed particularly suitable with regard to pliability or freedom from tendency to raggedness. On the contrary, the aspect of the linings is rather that of almost any piece to hand being thought sufficient for the purpose. The upper and lower blocks, cut from logs that had been standing for a long time and become attacked by insects, are shaped in his own way, that is, coming out further into the instrument and getting a better grip of upper and lower tables than is possible with the narrower ones used by Stradivari.

There is very little of any kind of finish about them,

the chippings of the gouge being very evident, and no traces of any glass-papering being present.

With regard to the surfaces of the upper and lower tables, these are mostly left quite even, probably being well rubbed down with glass paper. Atmospheric influence, combined with damp, has in almost all instances roughened the wood by causing the softer parts to swell.

The scraper does not appear to have been much used for the interior modelling of back and front, a small-toothed plane taking its place, very little trace of its work being left. Glass paper of different degrees of texture was doubtless much used, and the result is a much more finished condition than we might expect to have accompanied the rough gouging of the blocks and hasty trimming of the linings with a knife, of which there is evidence that it was of the pointed kind in use up to the present day.

The inner surfaces of the ribs are left at some places in the rough state as fresh from the saw, the marks of the teeth of which are plainly visible. The outside only received the perfect fining down and polished smoothness absolutely necessary as a foil for the highly-coloured lustrous varnish.

The parts of the blocks to which the ribs are attached are, as a matter of course, cut truly to the curves forming part of the design. Here we find again sufficient care and accuracy for an essentially important part of the whole. Neglect of proper precautions in gouging these portions of what may be termed the skeleton of the violin would result, as often as not, in bringing out quite a different outline when completed, or an entirely fresh type. The strictest attention is compulsory as to a careful continuation of the line or edge of the mould on to the corner and end blocks in accordance with the design.

In this respect the work of Joseph was as truly fitted as that of any other maker. All the blocks, before being detached from the mould and in their rough state, were of full average dimensions.

The following are the measurements of details of the interior of two late specimens—c. 1742-44, one in fresh condition excepting the modern bar and graft for lengthening the neck, the other in the state the maker left it, that is, with the old bar, neck, and original fingerboard.

No. 1, measured in the usual way, down the back from edge to edge, the length amounted to 14 in. bare by 8¼ in. greatest width.

The corner blocks across the top were unequal to each other, the upper left one being seven-eighths of an inch, the right thirteen-sixteenths. The lower left, one and a half, and the right, one and five-sixteenths. The parts where the linings are inserted at the waist curve are as a matter of course thicker, and in the manner of Stradivari, although rougher than his.

Why these blocks were unequal in their measurements must, in the absence of any precise indication, be left an open question. The upper block of semi-oval form was two inches across, with a projection of half an inch bare to the interior.

The lower one was one inch and three quarters, with a projection of nine-sixteenths of an inch; this is likewise semi-oval in the curving, but also roughly hewn.

The thickness of the back is greatest in the middle near the position of the soundpost, and is a quarter of an inch bare, gradually decreasing to an eighth near the linings all round.

The surface is well levelled, and does not give any indication of haste or want of proper care.

The join down the back is executed in a manner that cannot be excelled, the use of good tools and expert handling being strongly in evidence. All the backs, of the later period especially, that have come under my observation, have shown the same clean unsurpassable sharpness. Some that have the dark line at the join have been, perhaps from damp, open at some time, and have been closed up again by a repairer.

The front, in the one under consideration, is in one piece, excepting at the lower left side, where, the wood being insufficiently wide, it has an addition of about five eighths of an inch, to make up the deficiency, the thickness, about one sixteenth less than the back, graduating to the border in much the same manner.

It is not often that the upper table is made by Joseph of one piece only; frequently it is the other way, some being composed of four pieces.

The soundholes, of the long type favoured by the master in his late period, are bevelled round inside in the manner of Gasparo da Salo and Maggini; this must not be taken as invariably so; there may have been more than one reason for so doing. That it was in imitation of those masters seems quite unlikely, as there is nothing else in common between Joseph and the older Brescian makers.

The most probable reason seems to be that in the present instance, as in others of the same period, the bevelling was done for the purpose of relieving the edges of the soundholes of the very thick or clumsy aspect they would present if left in the usual way. Possibly other motives at the time lent their weight, and of which we now have no knowledge.

Of the No. 2, the following will give an idea of how Joseph varied in detail, or kept steadfastly in view certain mannerisms or rules for his own guidance. Length, measured as was No. 1, fourteen inches bare, by eight at greatest width.

The rise of the arching was a trifle less than in No. 1. Upper table in two parts; the lower likewise. Both finished or levelled in the same way, the lower table or back being at the same place a quarter of an inch full, declining to about one eighth near the linings. These latter were of the same materials and rough trimmings as of No. 1.

The lower corner blocks, measured as with No. 1, are equal with each other in size, one inch and a quarter; the upper ones also equal, one inch and three sixteenths, cut in precisely the same manner as those in No. 1.

The upper end block, one inch and three quarters, with a projection of five eighths into the interior, and of the same form. The lower one, one inch and five eighths, with a projection of five-eighths, roughly hewn to the same form as that of No. 1.

The soundholes of No. 2 are not bevelled like those of No. 1; they differ a little in size; the left one being three inches and a quarter bare, the right three inches and three sixteenths, as compared with those of No. 1, which measure, the left three inches and one eighth, the right three inches and three sixteenths.

The dimensions and position of the bar are as follows : length nine inches and three-quarters bare, depth five sixteenths full, width three sixteenths. Depth at each end one eighth, a little more at the lower end. It is cut, not as the moderns do, with the grain or threads upright, continuous with those of the table, but flat with it, that is, at right angles, and cut apparently from the same piece of pine as the table. This seems to have been a general custom with the Italian liutaros. It may have been a matter of convenience when there was a sufficiency of material at hand. It has a fair amount of finish, equal to that of the best of modern bars.

Some measurements of the exterior details of No. 2 may be interesting, from the rarity of specimens in their original condition, or as they left their maker's hands.

From top of scroll down to end, where it was glued outside the top ribs, which were not in this instance continuous, and further secured by the flat-headed nail driven into the block from the interior : from the end upwards to the opening of the peg-box, five inches less one-sixteenth. Total length of opening of peg-box, two inches and a half. Length of fingerboard, ten inches and one-eighth; width across top part, seven-eighths of an inch; lowest part, one inch and three-quarters.

Fingerboards on two others, made some fifteen years before, and giving the same measurements, were of pine, with a veneering of ebony. This seems to be some hint concerning the scarcity or expense of ebony for use in musical instruments at the time when Joseph Guarnerius was working.

There is further additional interest connected with No. 2 worth noticing, that is, the presence of the original tailpiece.

Nothing remarkable about that, we may fancy hearing said on this announcement, quite common no doubt; but there is something remarkable, inasmuch as the curves on each side of this detail, of no great importance, are more artistically curved than the modern type of manufactured article for utility only. We may fairly conclude that in the days of Joseph all the fittings were made by the maker of the instrument, or on the premises. Apart from the better and more graceful drawing, it is fashioned according to the old style in vogue before the introduction of the modern and so-called "secret tie," that is, it has two upright holes at the small end through which the tailstring passed, up one, over the top, then down again to the tailpin underneath, where it was tied or knotted.

It has a peculiarity that has not come under my notice before, that of being in two parts, of very good ebony, with the joint in the centre. The upper holes through which the ends of the four strings pass are a little closer together than is the case with the modern type, and no cross piece or ridge for the strings to pass over. The piercing of the holes is like that adopted at the present day. It is quite plain with the exception of a slight rut or groove all round by way of ornament.

In this tailpiece we have additional evidence of the scarcity or costliness of ebony at the time.

With equal good fortune in seeing the interior of an earlier type of Joseph's violin making, a few particulars in addition to the foregoing will be worthy of notice.

In this instance there is the same great thickness at the middle of the back or lower table. The upper, or pine table is, however, much less robust, although equal in thickness to the average of other makers of the time, that is to say, about one-ninth of an inch at thickest, or central portion, declining a little to the edges.

It may here be noted that according to the thickness

of each table, so the master exercised his judgment in treatment of detail; thus, with the thick backs or fronts, they being truly joined, it was not thought necessary to add any support. On the contrary, the last specimen referred to seemed to him as requiring some, as he added a strip of paper glued along the three joints of the upper table, this being of four pieces. In an early one of a different type the same treatment was noticeable.

One made during what some call his most careful, golden, or classical period (measurement of the thicknesses was not at the time of examination possible, although the upper table was reported as equal all over), had a strip of linen, or canvas for protecting or strengthening the back join. This method and material was in frequent use by different makers from the earliest days of the violin.

There is nothing in this practice that can be laid hold of as having in any way, mysterious or otherwise, a connection between the special quality or quantity of tone and its presence. There is no doubt about its having a muting or stifling effect if done to excess; all repairers or dealers of any experience are aware of this.

Joseph does not appear to have any time used studs, which modern repairers are addicted to, ofttimes to an excessive degree.

CHAPTER XVI.

Joseph's most Finished Period—His Flattest Modelling, His Refinement—The Gorgeousness of some Specimens—Joseph's Free Style at its Height—His Purfling at Times—His Purfling Tool.

HAVING now considered the general arrangements of the interior of Joseph Guarnerius's violins of different dates, we may resume our study of the period that according to some admirers was his grandest or golden period. If excellence in mechanical neatness is to be the criterion, then it will be confessedly his best. 1733 to 1736 may be classed under that heading. The violins sent forth during these years may, in almost all respects, lay claim to as high a standard of finish as the majority of the efforts of the Amatis or Stradivari.

Some intention of neatness or accuracy of carving even in the volutes of the scroll is observable, but there is an almost corresponding decline in the force or strength of expression in this part.

With certainty it may be urged that the forms, both as regards the outline all round and of the soundholes, are such as do not seem possible to excel in gracefulness. The waist curves, although of large development (the grand, long inner bouts, as they have been called by a writer of eminence), are absolutely free from hardness of expression. The line of general contour is conducted round with a tenderness that seems to be the result of a careful calculation of every fractional portion. The purfling, although still showing Joseph's peculiar method

of handling, cannot be said to be inferior to that of any
other master.   The soundholes, cut with a decision of
purpose, combined with the greatest freedom, are
certainly equal, mechanically considered, to any work
in the same direction that had been seen before ; in fact,
with the precision and classic quality of Antonio
Stradivari he combined more energy, or as some express
it, " more go."

A large majority of these instruments are in length a
trifle under fourteen inches—it may be said they are
nearly always so ; they are of full width, that is, eight to
eight and a quarter across the lower part.   This proportion being so frequent, it has almost become a recognized
size for a Joseph, but, as with most details in connection
with his work, we may look out for surprises, and be
suddenly confronted with an instrument the proportions
of which are different.

Why this proportion was so often adhered to is
impossible to point out with any certainty; the requirements of Joseph's patrons in the direction of taste
or fancy were perhaps satisfied better with the bare
fourteen inches or an eighth under, although the
difference in the length of stop, or that which might be
perceptible in the handling of the body of the instrument,
is so small as to be almost unnoticeable among players
of the present day.   The period from 1730 to 1738 is
marked by the general lowness of the arching, or, as it is
so frequently called, the flat model, and by the public
supposed to be Joseph's distinguishing characteristic
innovation.   It was not his alone, however, as Lorenzo
Guadagnini had been working on a system of modelling
quite as low in the arching, and therefore taking likewise
a correspondingly short soundpost.

But Joseph, although using as low an arching as any
of Lorenzo's, seems, very seldom like that master, to have
made the very large or Maggini-proportioned violins,
which in most instances have a reduced height for the
ribs all round.

It has been asserted that there are some violins of

Plate XXXVI.
VIOLIN, JOSEPH GUARNERIUS, C. 1740.

Plate XXXVII.
VIOLIN, JOSEPH GUARNERIUS, 1740.

Plate XXXVIII.
VIOLIN, JOSEPH GUARNERIUS, C. 1740. SCROLL.

Plate XXXIX.
VIOLIN, JOSEPH GUARNERIUS, C. 1740. SCROLL.

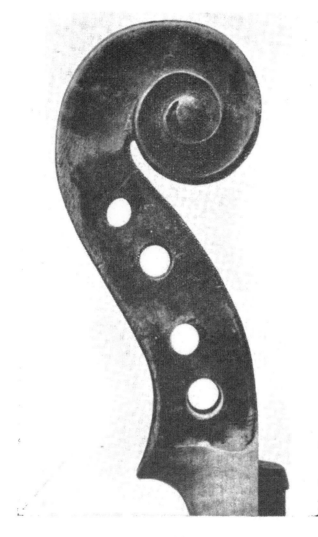

Plate XL.
VIOLIN, JOSEPH GUARNERIUS, C. 1740.   SCROLL.

Joseph's work that are perfectly flat, but they have not come under my notice as yet, and I am inclined to doubt the existence of any that can be classed as such in its absolute sense. A level surface would not be compatible with the artistic tastes of such a master of arts as Joseph Guarnerius was now proving himself to be.

Having now been for years busily occupied in the pursuit of his art, in close proximity with long-established veterans, some of whom seem to have in no lessened degree inherited the talent and retained in full the reputation of their family for the highest class of workmanship, it seems to be in accordance with the natural order of things that there would be points of detail about them that might serve the purpose of Joseph in improving his own work. It has already been noticed that, like many masters in other art works, he was on the alert to seize and apply for his own use any little touches in the work of men around him that seemed to him worthy of annexation. With these accepted hints, or ideas that might at different times arise therefrom, his style as a whole was getting more in conformity with that which was most fashionable around him—in short he may be said to have been getting more into what has since become recognized as the distinctly Cremonese style. This may be summed up in contradistinction to and priority over other schools as displaying the combination of excellence and originality of design, efforts at obtaining elegance of form, and richness of colour, with the highest order of tone quality.

He had all along been in possession of the last; and of colour for some time. At present he was working out his ideal of the best violin form with a measure of success that was to be judged of more completely by after generations. But he was now adding some of that kind of finish and delicacy of treatment in detail for which the city of Cremona had for generations held the highest position, and become celebrated wherever the violin was known.

The lines forming the pattern were having increased

o

attention in their direction and firmness of drawing; ruggedness such as he had delighted in for many years was to be put aside; the knife work was effected with an earnestness and intensity of thought that was bound to draw attention from the individuality of it alone; acknowledgment of excellence would follow as a matter of course.

These two items in the summary of results, accruing from earnest endeavours at accomplishing the really highest class of work, were in the greatest degree of probability mainly due to the near presence of old Antonio Stradivari and his sons.

An examination of, or frequent contact with the gems of art sent forth from the house of that master, without doubt prompted the idea of affixing some of the touches, which in Joseph's perception, would, without harm to his own style, be an enhancement of the general effect.

Resulting from this we find the cleanly cut, piquantly designed, and beautifully finished soundholes gracing the period from 1733 to nearly 1740.

For some years previously hints had been thrown out as to what might be likely to be produced in the future. Anyone prognosticating that the apparent impossibility of producing soundholes having the classic proportions and elegance (for so many years placed before the admiring eyes of the cognoscenti of Cremona) would be really overcome, might have seen his predictions verified in the designs now produced.

In comparison with those of Stradivari, the very finished soundholes of Joseph Guarnerius of the 1733 to 1738 period have all the excellencies of the first with a trifle more energy of expression; the upper holes are a degree larger, as are the lower ones very slightly. There is less flow or bend over at each end of the main opening, although this is managed with such dexterity of drawing that there is no loss of grace, but on the contrary, there seems to be an advance in that direction. A straight line drawn from end to end will show a slight increase in the length.

The expression of strength in the soundholes is thus intensified, and their individuality augmented.

During the progress of these modifications of style, slight as they may appear, other portions of the work that would go for helping in the general effect of magnificence were kept well in view. The sycamore has evidently been selected for its handsome figure ; sometimes, the backs being in one piece, the broad curls appear as if suddenly streaked across from side to side in a careless manner, the so-called "nutmeggy" aspect of the grain being brought out conspicuously by the very vivid hues of the varnish.

These occasionally have a very daring look, that is, a near approach, but kept within bounds, to gaudiness ; a step further, we might say, would be ruinous. This degree, however, was exactly where the genius of the master was emphatically proved to be present. Constant repetition of tint was not at all to the taste of Joseph, nor has it been so with other masters of the art.

Sometimes the sycamore is of closer curl, although it may have been from the same tree, or others growing close by ; it has, however, under the master's treatment, been made to present the same kind of glorious aspect, when under the brilliant orange-coloured varnish, of having been bathed in liquid transparent gold.

I remember many years back, when a connoisseur was inspecting in rapt admiration an orange-coloured Joseph which had been brought for his inspection, his exclamation on turning it about, "Why, the varnish seems all alive ! " It cannot be for a moment contended that the gorgeous envelope endowed with such quality could have been the result of either accident, haphazard experiment, or mere dashing workmanship; in art this does not occur, however swiftly the actual handiwork is accomplished—if it is of the highest class. It is only produced after much earnest effort in former days, the final ripe results having followed in their right and appropriate turn.

Were it possible to get details of the working life of

Joseph Guarnerius, all the indications that we can perceive in his work of this period would doubtless be in harmony with the hypothesis that at this time he was in possession of a fine stock of specially-selected materials, and that his patronage was such as made him what people nowadays would call comfortably off.

We now come to another, or what might be called a semi-period, as the materials, and in most instances the work, is similar, although there is a change; not a sudden one, but intermixed with the type referred to above there are those which have been described by a well-known connoisseur as "impudent fiddles"—not a bad expression, when the instruments are taken consecutively and mentally analysed.

These are the works that, when put forward by Joseph in the plenitude of his powers and ripened experience, were to be viewed by connoisseurs of future ages as masterpieces left by the great exponent of free style in the liutaro's art. By this we must understand, as Joseph has shown in his work, that it was independence and freedom from the shackles of hard and fast rules under which so many liutaros had laboured hitherto. The types and individual works that were now about to be sent forth, impressed some connoisseurs of the last century as having so much freedom and apparently so little consideration as to suggest the possibility of his violins having been made, not in the ordinary way—on the block or mould—but all the parts built one to another as the work progressed.

This, however, is not in the least degree likely, there being, in fact, ample evidence against it, perceptible to the connoisseur who can claim to have a practical knowledge of the subject.

The variety of design as regards outline or pattern, the difference in the rise and detailed curving of the arching or modelling, the apparently inexhaustible store of ideas concerning the drawing or cutting of the sound-holes, as well as those masterpieces of carving—the scrolls, all point emphatically to the possession by the artist of a fecund strength of artistic faculty and perception of what was sure to impress the minds of his future critics. This caused him to stand alone in many respects, and in others as the rival of Antonio Stradivari.

The period 1738, and after, stands in the minds of many of Joseph's admirers as possibly his best.

His powers by this time were fully matured; he had initiated a style, essentially his own, now associated with his name, imitations since appearing having the more salient points emphasized, as is commonly done.

His violins of this period have wonderful variety of expression depicted over the design, and have each an individualism distinct enough for general recognition, many specimens being known under different nicknames, given by owners and connoisseurs, often no doubt with very slender foundation, the enthusiastic admiration of the owner for the more striking qualities as regards style and colour suggesting some out of the way name by which the particular instrument may be known in the future. The stamp of the master hand is perceptible over all the work sent out, each piece, although being a variation upon what had gone before, having the characteristic touch of the artist, evincing a facile independent handling of the work, a kind that had never been seen before, and which has not been repeated since. The great mastery of the subject is more evident when we take in review some of the efforts in the way of free style by makers who deigned to follow in the same path.

Among them Laurentius Storioni (working afterwards in the same city) stands out prominently, a man of strong points of excellence, and whose works have been often confused with those of Joseph Guarnerius, and not unfrequently sold as his.

A careful comparison of the peculiarities of each, especially with regard to the flow of line and details in general, will bring to the eye of the connoisseur much that will show to advantage the qualities of refinement on the part of Joseph. No matter with how much vigorous treatment, boldness, or eccentricity he may have invested his work, it will be found accompanied by an air of daintiness and elegance, which if not altogether absent in the work of his followers or imitators, is many degrees beyond all their efforts.

The details catching the eye first were those particularly paid attention to by the imitators of Joseph, early and late. Thus the soundholes were cut in what is frequently called the "Gothic style," or pointed arch manner, and usually exaggerated with regard to the form at each end. Trying to make sure that these parts would attract the eye of the connoisseur, there was the hope that once recognising them as a favourite fancy of Joseph, the examiner would rest content and not proceed further.

The really pointed form of soundholes, that is with a distinctly sharp pointed arch form, is foreign to Joseph. Where these do appear on his work, they will be found on close inspection to have been touched up by some later hand, who, fearful that the work would not be recognisable by every one at a glance, added what seemed to him to be the necessary additional touch to make it so.

Taking the period we have been considering, and up to the last, as being better included as one, there are a few particulars that might be with advantage brought to notice.

Joseph had for some years been, what some people call "thoroughly himself," or his peculiarities and fancies allowed to go free to the full extent of his judgment. Some of these have been referred to, others we may now take note of.

As usual with other artists and craftsmen, the age of the worker was like enough to impress itself in some way or other on his work. Irregular, spasmodic, and fanciful as Joseph's work had appeared so often through the whole of his career, there was one detail in which there was more steadiness of handling at the end than at the beginning. This was with regard to the insertion of the purfling.

During the time extending over the years 1733 to 1740
(*See Plates XXXVI., XXXVII., XXXVIII., XXXIX.,
and XL.*), his powers of mechanical neatness were at
their best, or it may be said that he exercised them with
more earnest attention. In his latest period there does
not appear to be any falling off in power, but there is
some suggestion about the work that the necessity for
neatness was not so urgent. A few hints appear to have
been thrown out at times of a gradual increase in heavi-
ness of style. Some connoisseurs have admired this,
but we can leave the fact alone in its relation to the
latest period of the great maker's life.

It is in the management of the purfling that the vast
hordes of copyists, good, bad or indifferent, meet with
their greatest stumbling block. There is the same
obstacle to success in copying Joseph as in making a
correct facsimile of the work of Gasparo da Salo.

Each of the masters had his own method, peculiar,
fanciful, or native, as may appear most appropriate
terms ; both occasionally seeming very hasty, and at
times very leisurely, in their progress through this part
of the work, and neither giving the spectator the impression that the maker thought it a detail of superior
importance.

That they did attach some, if not considerable, weight
to this part of the enrichment of the whole design, is
evident to some degree by the fact of their never
omitting it as many makers did.

It is the presence of this simple little fillet, composed
mostly of three pieces of wood glued together, the
outer ones being dark, sometimes black, and the middle
of some light coloured wood, both kinds selected according to fancy, convenience or necessity, that gives the
look of finish or completeness. Some makers having
once decided on a certain combination of woods for
effect, kept strictly to the same materials and manner
throughout their career ; others for a time only, and then
changed or adopted another kind occasionally.

Perhaps of no maker can it be said that one

style, size, and exact identity of material characterised his work at all times. With Stradivari the fancy in early times was for the outer or dark parts to be cut from some very black and hard material, possibly ebony. The same may be said of his son Francesco's early work. This was suitable for very slow, highly finished work. In this respect Stradivari was following in the steps of his teacher, Nicolas Amati.

Joseph Guarnerius in like manner followed for a time in the path of his eccentric instructor, but, his natural independence soon asserting itself, there was a rapidly developed style of his own brought before the public eye.

Following the comparatively coarse and careless manner of Andreas Gisalberti, there was in the large work or full sized violins by Joseph Guarnerius a leaning towards looseness and want of regularity, that would strike many connoisseurs, seeing it for the first time, as more like a very old man's work than that of a young tyro on the threshold of what was to be a remarkable career.

That the want of pliability in the material used for purfling had caused him some thought is evidenced by the central portion, or light coloured wood, being, in some rather early instances, cut with the grain aslant and not running continuously with the outer or dark line. He seems to have soon given this up and returned to the usual manner of cutting the material, as if the advantages did not balance well with the increase of limpness.

Among the more finished or delicately worked instruments of 1734 to 1738 the composition of the purfling is of materials that were not very striking with regard to the contrast between themselves or to the work of masters working in the neighbourhood.

The succeeding years witnessed an increase in the colour of the dark wood, till at the last part of his career, at the consideration of which we have now arrived, it is nearer in tint to black than at any other time. It does not give any indication of failing power, steadiness, or strength, and has been inserted in the same manner as at the outset of his career.

All through it may noticed that he firstly used what is known as a double purfling tool, that is the two lines first cut to serve as a guide for cutting the groove were made simultaneously, and not as by some makers, one line at a time; precisely the same rule was followed by Gasparo da Salo.

Taking now into consideration the latest part of Joseph's career, we may draw a comparison between it and the one preceding. The length of the soundholes is ' retained, also their relative position with regard to the design. The pattern varies, it might almost be said with each one, but the style is retained.

The waist curves are not so long as had been often made by him in 1734 and sometime afterwards, there are some suspicions aroused as to a tendency to return, willingly or not, to the ruggedness of earlier days, though to a modified extent.

The rise of the model varies also, but not upwards to any considerable extent. The channelling is of a very trifling depth, next to nothing it may be called. There is, as usual with Joseph, variety in this part of the construction. In one instance known to me (possibly others may be extant) there is an elevation near all the four corners back and front, a little above the upper, likewise beneath the lower ones, where usually the slight hollowing at the angle is the termination of the channelling. On passing the finger over these four parts the slight rise or prominence is distinctly felt, and seen also when the instrument is moved about in the light; it might be taken as an accidental peculiarity but for the presence of it at all the other angles. I have met with the same peculiarity in a large pattern Lorenzo Guadagnini violin of the period of Maggini influence. Who first introduced this peculiarity, or whether either saw the other, it would be interesting to know.

The size of these late Josephs varies, although but a

trifle, but the full fourteen inches in length is more frequently met with than before.

Like other masters of his time, Joseph Guarnerius made extra sized' ones occasionally, but here the habits and customs of the army of dealers step in to interfere with their coming into the broad sunlight for admiration and discussion as to the relative degrees of excellency.

There was much prejudicial criticism handed about when the mathematical proportion and air-space theorists were disseminating their doctrines, as to the absolute necessity of a certain number of millimetres this or that way, and exactly corresponding cubic measurements inside for air space being likewise imperative, and that the construction of a perfect violin, in addition to the compulsory usage of certain woods for back and front, demanded that these should give precisely a tone different to each other when tested according to the methods adopted by these pseudo discoverers of the profound secret of the master liutaros of Italy.

The ideas thus promulgated had their day, like most others which have in the same direction proved effete, and the world at large has passed them over, securing, when practicable, any specimens that may by chance turn up, and valuing them according to their good qualities and preservation.

CHAPTER XVII.

JOSEPH'S LATE VARNISH AND THAT OF HIS CONTEM-
PORARIES IN OTHER PLACES, DIFFERENCE BETWEEN
IT AND HIS EARLIER KIND—THE DECADENCE OF
THE ITALIAN VARNISHES GENERALLY—THEIR PECU-
LIARITIES AND DIFFERENCES OF MATERIAL—HIS
SYCAMORE BORED BY INSECTS—HIS EFFORT TO
SAVE AND NOT THROW AWAY HIS WORK.

A FEW further remarks concerning Joseph's varnish,
especially during his late period.

When first emerging into public life as an
Italian master liutaro, as has before been noticed, his
varnish was not of the precise quality of that used by
his teacher Andreas Gisalberti. Why, there is no available evidence.

As he progressed he appears to have changed his ideas
as to the colour and consistency, perhaps as circumstances were favourable to one or another; chiefly, however, the range seems to have been among the yellow, or
transparent ochre tints and light brown. After a while,
in conjunction with his namesake, he seems to have
become aware of the advantage of putting more intense
colour into the varnish over his now varying works.
Further developments culminated in the brilliant finish
or clothing of the entire work, which, with other high
qualities, were to be the means of placing their author
upon the highest pinnacle of fame. There was to be yet
another change, and in this there is as much mystery as
in the composition in other respects of the most glorious
varnish ever used by the Italian masters.

It must be noticed here that at the period 1742, or a little later, there were some not very obscure signs on the horizon, of the approaching decadence in the art of the Italian liutaro, taken as a whole, and in particular, that of the final disappearance of the famous inimitable varnishes and the method of their application.

Old Antonio Stradivari had been dead some years. There is some uncertainty as to either of his sons, Francesco or Omobono, using, as late as 1740, the old classic material and method, if indeed they were actually continuing their work so late. Their father's last works were very likely entirely varnished by them.

As to Carlo Bergonzi's use of the splendid recipe up to this time, there is also much room for doubt.

The great Venetian masters, Gobetti and Montagnana, at about the same time, were, in combination it might almost be said, giving forth to the world of liutaros and their admirers unmistakeable indications that henceforward there would be a cessation of the issue of those rich or gorgeous coatings that had been for more than a century a distinguishing feature of the works of the principal Italian liutaros. The question naturally following, Why? brings us to the consideration of what facts are at our disposal concerning the output of Joseph Guarnerius and his contemporaries.

Mr. Honeyman's violin is of bold design, the treatment of the border, which is rather broad, and the corners being suggestive of the manner of Gisalberti. The modelling is of gentle rise and the sides or ribs of full average height. The back is of one piece of his boldly figured sycamore, the curls declining from left to right. It will be seen that the waist curves do not appear so extended as the 1734-38 types. The scroll (not represented) is of full size, and the side view shows the curve of the grooves running down to the shell very full, the gouging of the turns being executed in the usual masterly manner. Length 14in., greatest width $8\frac{1}{8}$ in.

Miss Eveline Petherick's Joseph Guarnerius belongs to a type, or it might be termed a batch, sent forth at the

MR. W. C. HONEYMAN'S JOSEPH GUARNERIUS, C. 1742.

MISS EVELINE PETHERICK'S JOSEPH GUARNERIUS, C. 1738.

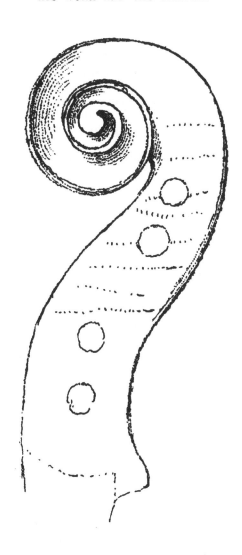

SCROLL OF MISS PETHERICK'S
JOSEPH GUARNERIUS, 1738.

same period as the "King Joseph" that passed through
the hands of the late D. Laurie. It is deep orange in
colour, the purfling carefully inserted and ending at the
corners in a long point in both violins, probably others of
the same group are extant. In the present instance the
cloud, stain or smoke line, whatever we may term it, is
distinctly seen. The tone is of great brilliance and
carrying power. Length 13¾ in., greatest width 8⅛ in.
full.

The first point is that all the leading masters seem
to have been showing the same signs, and the same
degree in kind, of decadence in the varnishing branch
of their art.

A writer has observed that the celebrated and wonderful Italian varnish was disappearing, whether from
inability, carelessness, or great costliness, no one knew,
but that it was likely enough that the great man, Joseph
Guarnerius, was the first to start the fall, as with the oft
repeated simile of the pack of cards.

In this there is one mistake most apparent, namely,
that of arguing upon the old assumption that the varnishing was nothing more or less than a mere painting over
the work with some beautiful transparent liquid, at one
time easy to get and apply, but possibly tedious in
drying, and therefore too costly in working. This simple
hypothesis, with insufficient basis, could not have been
the result of long and good practical acquaintance with
the contemporary makers of the time, or with Joseph
Guarnerius in particular; a careful analysis of all
possible facts in connection with the subject leads to the
conclusion that "Joseph's varnish," like all the fine
varnishes of the Brescian, Cremonese, Venetian, and
other Italian schools, was of two or more kinds quite
distinct in their nature, ingredients, and application; that
each of these was not one simple solution only, but
several; that at the time now under consideration, one of
the ingredients of the upper, or more intensely coloured
films, was the first to go, and was not obtainable either
in Cremona, Venice, or other centres of the art.

The reasons for this conclusion are, that the lowest coats, or priming, in Joseph's late work, like that of the other masters referred to, appeared to be quite as brilliant, if not more so, over the freshly tooled work as at any previous time.

The upper coats have less brilliancy and transparency, and seem actually less firm in substance than before.

Much the same peculiarities characterise the work produced at the same time in Venice by Gobetti, Montagnana and the Tononis, besides makers of less note at other places.

The mode in which the top varnish of these makers aged, or oxidized, as time progressed, was similar to that of Joseph. The contraction of the materials was of a kind different from that of former times; then it had a look as from a gentle heating causing a fine frizzle, now it was of a larger texture showing a kind of inter-lacing of sharp incisions with a raised central portion caused by the contraction.

To dive in among the researches necessary for arriving at any sort of conclusion as to the causes of this appear-ance and process of contraction as time progressed, would lead us too far from our course.

That Joseph Guarnerius, besides other makers of less repute, would have continued the use of the "glorious envelope," if it had been possible, we may take for granted, as it is difficult to conceive of any possible change of fashion or growing dislike to the artistically rich colour and transparency of aspect that had been associated with the works of the principal liutaros of the Italian centres of the art.

The difference noticeable on the late productions of the above mentioned master does not refer alone to that of consistency or identity of material, but to the apparent increase in the difficulty of application. On a close examination of untouched varnish on a Joseph Guarnerius, 1735, likewise on a Carlo Bergonzi of about the same period, there was distinct evidence of the upper or last coats of varnish having been applied with a brush,

P

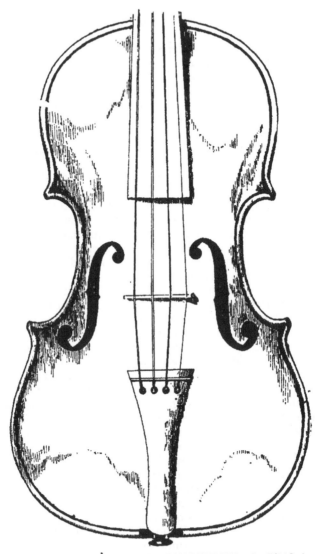

H. PETHERICK'S JOSEPH GUARNERIUS, C. 1742-4.
RUBY BROWN COLOUR.
This violin is of slightly higher elevation than many of this period.

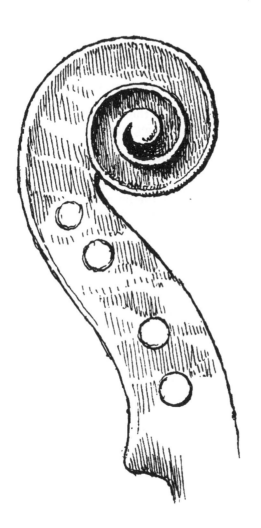

SCROLL OF H. PETHERICK'S
JOSEPH GUARNERIUS, 1742-4.

P 2

probably of fine hog hair, of about a quarter of an inch wide, without any after rubbing down or polishing.

Of this I have not been able to trace anything in the very late productions of Joseph, which helps to some degree the hypothesis that one of the components or methods which had been in constant use was not now in evidence.

Further than this, to obtain the colour, or a reasonable substitute for the missing ingredient, a thicker film seemed necessary.

There are the same difficulties in the way of arriving at a conclusion as to the composition of the late varnish as an early one ; time has laid its hand on both, and as years went by after the decease of the liutaros, the atmospheric operations upon the works were more indelibly marked.

There appears at present no possibility of science coming to our aid during the investigation of the composition of the varnish. The application of different gums or resins from unknown sources, more or less acted upon by the atmosphere, is the only result unfolded to us by the researches of the analytical chemist. The colours of the varnishes on the latest of Joseph's works vary, but they are mostly of brownish hue.

The thicker consistence of the varnish, placed over work that is on the whole of a bolder type than that of a few years previous, adds to the general effect of massiveness. There may be in the opinion of some critics less grace and delicacy, but they will admit there is an increase in force of character. The long waist curves are modified and of the average length. The rise of the arching is about the same as before, with occasional exceptions, as might be expected.

In the carving of the scrolls there is the same untrammelled independence of idea as before, the size varying apparently with the humour of the moment, but there is always that strong energetic expression in the design, which is carried out with a very deep gouging, impressing the spectator of it as having been accomplished by a strong hand.

There are a few further remarks that may be made concerning the late types of Joseph's scrolls and necks, when the latter are entire, giving indication of their having been cut from a store of sycamore that had been bored by insects, or as it is commonly expressed had " got the worm in it." The storing of the sycamore, selected on account of its suitable quality in the judgment of Joseph a great number of years back, was, particularly in somewhat confined back premises, or in the small yard, very liable to such attacks, and as all violin makers are aware, the extent of the boring is frequently only discovered when much of the work has been accomplished, so Joseph working at his splendid figured sycamore, came upon unanticipated depredations of these nuisances to the liutaro, and was forced either to put aside the half carved back or scroll, or plug the holes. That this was the case is shown in several instances in which a hole has been plugged each side of the central line, the half table having been in the usual way sawn through and the thick sides brought together for joining, and thus disclosing holes each side level with each other.

Other instances there are where Joseph has, on gouging the volutes of the scroll, come upon a number of holes clustered together, or confluent, but setting too high a value upon his work already done, he has preferred a considerable amount of plugging, to putting it aside as labour lost.

The evidence of this treatment is in the fact that the varnish in its original state has been carried over the pluggings, which, moreover, have been done with pieces from the same log as the surrounding wood.

The pine appears to be of the same quality as used by Joseph for many years, or throughout his career. The late works have pine with quite as much refinement of texture, and the acoustical properties are quite up to his old standard, if not a trifle in advance with regard to brilliancy, and what is known as "spreading quality."

That these two qualities were the ones desirable

among the increasing numbers of the violinists of the
time, and afterwards, there cannot be any doubt
During the latter half of Joseph's career it will be found
by those having the means of examination, that Carlo
Bergonzi now and then turned out instruments of
penetrative power much beyond that usual with him, and
further, Francesco Stradivari went more thoroughly into
the matter, and, so far as I have been able to ascertain,
permanently adopted a higher keynote or register for
his violins, but not quite so high as that always
adopted by Joseph Guarnerius, who in this respect kept
on the level of the first three Amatis, although obtaining,
by means of his own, greatly increased volume of tone.

These contemporary masters, however, in these
instances were not so happy in their results; in supply-
ing the quality of increased brilliancy they were in
danger of lessening other equally essential ones.

Of the conclusion of the career of Joseph Guarnerius
there is at present a want of data in connection therewith, those who had been successful to some extent in
obtaining useful particulars regarding the details of his
relationship with other members of the somewhat
numerous family, having been unable to arrive with
certainty as to the exact year of his demise. It is
generally placed at 1745 or 1746.

CHAPTER XVIII.

WHETHER JOSEPH MADE MANY VIOLAS—ONE WITH THE
LADY'S NAME AS MAKER—THE MYSTERIOUS I.H.S.
SOLVED—GENERAL REVIEW OF JOSEPH'S WORKING
CAREER.

WHETHER Joseph Guarnerius at any time made violas and violoncellos is an inquiry often made, but up to the present time one only has been seen by me, although I have heard of others having been seen in Italy. This, however, is by no means to be taken as final evidence, as the violoncello by Gisalberti alluded to shows. I have only recently been able to examine the viola illustrated in the book by the late Mr. G. Hart, and found it very interesting, not as a Joseph, but Carlo Bergonzi of a type before referred to, when he imitated Joseph's free style. With regard to the making of violas as a regular practice, there is what might be taken as indirect evidence.

Some years back, when in London, I was informed of a viola which might interest me, and which being in the neighbourhood my informant kindly had it brought for my inspection. The ticket inside in legible characters was as follows :—

KATARINA GUARNERIA FECIT ✠
CREMONE ANNO 1749.   I.H.S.

A continental dealer who happened to be present said

he had met with two violins abroad with similar tickets, both having a fine tone.

On scrutinizing the details, I remarked that Joseph's actual workmanship was not evident, but that of some other hand, and that a fair conclusion would be that the viola was made after Joseph's decease. The date is in agreement with this possibility, someone being perhaps employed by Katarina Guarnerius, who, if his widow, was keeping on the business while the stock of precious materials lasted and employed an assistant.

It was interesting to find that the soundholes, although not cut by Joseph, seemed as if traced from one of his early patterns, during the Gisalberti influence. They may have been used for the present purpose without knowledge of there being any others of later date, or existent.

In the above quoted ticket there appears a detail of some interest, as it will be observed that the cross with I.H.S. below is placed as on Joseph's tickets.

There has been much meditation over this, some thinking it to have some mysterious signification, or that the master belonged to some secret guild or possibly prohibited society. The fact of the above ticket, with others having the same signature, seems to point more emphatically to its having been only a monogram of Joseph's fancy for emphasis alone, and that his widow (if she was so) kept it on the tickets for recognition for the few years after her husband's decease.

There was a Hieronymus Guarnerius working in Cremona about the same time and later, and this may have seemingly helped the apparent necessity. Of this maker at present there are no details available.

Many spurious instruments, among them violas, have come before me, with the one result of showing each artificer in the light of making ludicrous experiments.

In a book illustration of a viola attributed to the great master it did not appeal to my judgment as being a veritable work of his, the contour seeming too much of a departure from the native inclinations of Joseph to be in any way a help in the matter. Had he taken up the construction of the viola as part of his regular daily work, I think there would have been extant sufficient evidence of it.

With regard to violoncellos also the same may be said. Like the first great master of the art, Gasparo da Salo, Joseph Guarnerius may have taken to the special line of making violins almost exclusively, being sufficiently occupied therewith to his satisfaction, and without ambition to gain further laurels in other directions. This conclusion, however, may have to be set aside at any moment owing to instruments turning up, as in the case of his master before referred to.

From the foregoing particulars of the working career of Joseph Guarnerius, it will be gathered that so far from being the erratic and spasmodic artist of genius, commencing his career at a time of life usually accompanied by permanently settled associations, we have the presentation of a young student leaving his master's atelier with the usual priming of method and manner of work, and from which was gradually evolved his own.

Thus as time went on, having thrown aside almost entirely the influence of his master, Gisalberti, his own style having matured, he, working in the midst of the classical scholars of the period, infused into his own productions the selected portions of their style that seemed to him sufficiently worthy of attachment, and sent forth to the world those works which were in future times to bring him an imperishable reputation as one of the two greatest masters of the liutaro's art, and in honourable rivalry with the other, Antonio Stradivari, with whom the name of Joseph Guarnerius is always associated.

In reviewing briefly the working career of Joseph Guarnerius as a now universally acknowledged great master without a superior, it may be asked why and in what especial particular he has merited this high position. The answer is threefold and decisive, firstly, on account of the tone quality of his instruments; secondly, the form; and thirdly, the quality of varnish.

Of the three important and indispensable qualifications that go for the making of a masterpiece of violin making, that of tone must necessarily take the first place, inasmuch as the instrument comes before the public for competition with others chiefly as a means of making beautiful sounds. From the first start off Joseph coupled clearness and volume together, and it was doubtless with much consideration of the tone produced by his teacher Gisalberti that he decided to continue in the same course with regard to the full soprano "timbre," the quality that the Amatis favoured, and to which Joseph, while retaining the refinement and sympathetic qualities, added greatly increased power. No maker seems more regular in the production of the same peculiarity of tone; once understood he is found to be definitely separated from other tone masters. His power of producing the individuality or character of tone quality seems to have remained unimpaired to the last; rather was the brilliancy or spreading peculiarity increased than otherwise during his latest period, and to which the instrument belonged that was played upon by the greatest of all virtuosi, while the renown of both appears as fairly equally divided.

It will be seen that from the first we know of him his efforts were continuous and ardent toward accomplishing a design that would take a position as a classical one, and be recognised as containing among the excellencies the necessary elements of simplicity and grace. After many years struggling with details apparently trifling in themselves, but which were unavoidably attached to the varied modification of each idea, he arrived at the goal of his ambition, producing what the world now well knows as the Joseph Guarnerius pattern, as distinct as that of any master who preceded him, and which for simple elegance has not been excelled. This design may be said to have been at its greatest perfection from the year 1733 to 1740. During this time the mechanical dexterity shown over the work was equal to most of that put forward by the great master and near neighbour of his,

Antonio Stradivari.   With the efforts at improvement
in form there was the more sudden development in
richness of effect in the varnish as regards colour, this
being striking in its splendour and artistic quality.

That Joseph Guarnerius was an industrious worker is
evidenced by the large number of instruments now extant
showing his individual handiwork.   There is little or
nothing about them suggestive of the assistance or help
of any workman ; almost as a matter of course we must
take it that he did have help, but it could only have been
in the larger or coarser handling of the work ; all details
that call the attention of the connoisseur are invariably
his.

Of the makers reputed to have been pupils of
Joseph Guarnerius there are but two; first of whom
stands Lorenzo Storioni, who has a renown for tone in
Italy, which is strong evidence of his merits.   His
earliest date of working, referring to his tickets known
at present, is 1741, the tone of his violins proclaims him
to be of the Joseph Guarnerius school, being large and
clear but not so sympathetic.   His workmanship is bold
and in many respects resembles that of Joseph, but
when compared with him Storioni is much less refined ;
he apparently, unlike his supposed teacher, never made
any attempts at elegance of contour.   His varnish from
first to last is of the kind known as alcoholic, and seems
of one consistency, possibly of the same number of coats.

His tickets do not, to my knowledge, at any time
mention his having been a pupil of Joseph.   The
materials used by him vary much, especially that of the
backs which seem to indicate much hunting in out of the
way places ; it is occasionally of curious figure, sometimes
very plain.   He has been frequently sold as Joseph
Guarnerius, but however much he may to the in-
experienced eye resemble that master, in all essential
particulars, especially tone, he is quite independent.

The other name is that of Pietro Falco, 1764, whose
ticket, I have been informed, says he was pupil of
Joseph Guarnerius, but as I have not become acquainted

with more than one instrument of his, and that many
years back, there are not enough data concerning him at
my command; the recollection of the instrument is not
of its belonging to the school of Guarnerius, and those
who are said to have seen his work describe it as of
Stradivarian tendencies.

There is the possibility of the Hieronymus Guarnerius
mentioned before being of the family, and continuing the
business under the name of Katarina Guarnerius, but we
cannot say more.

[The End.]

"THE STRAD" LIBRARY, No. II.

Crown 8vo., Cloth, 2/6, Post Free, 2/9.

HOW TO STUDY THE VIOLIN
By J. T. CARRODUS.

CONTENTS.

Strings and Tuning. The Bow and Bowing. Faults and their Correction. Scales and their Importance. Course of Study. Advice on Elementary Matters. Concerning Harmonics, Octaves, etc. Orchestral Playing. Some Experiences as a Soloist. With full page portraits of Carrodus, Molique, Paganini, Spohr, Sivori, De Beriot, Blagrove and Sainton, and a photo-reproduction of Dr. Spohr's testimonial to Carrodus.

"An interesting series of articles ' How to Study the Violin,' which Carrodus contributed to THE STRAD, and completed only a week or two before his death, have now been collected in cheap book form. The technical hints to violin students, which are practical, plainly worded, and from such a pen most valuable."—*Daily News.*

" But a few weeks before his sudden death the most distinguished of native violinists completed in THE STRAD a series of chats to students of the instrument associated with his name. These chats are now re-issued, with a sympathetic preface and instructive annotations. All who care to listen to what were virtually the last words of such a conscientious teacher will recognise the pains taken by Carrodus to render every detail as clear to the novice as to the advanced pupil. Pleasant gossip concerning provincial festivals at which Carrodus was for many years ' leader ' of the orchestra, ends a little volume worthy a place in musical libraries both for its practical value and as a memento of the life-work of an artist universally esteemed.''—*Daily Chronicle.*

" It is surely, hardly necessary to direct the attention of students to the unique value of the hints and advice given by so experienced and accomplished a virtuoso as the late Mr. Carrodus, so that it only remains to state that the ' Recollections ' make delightful reading, and that the book, as a whole, is as entertaining as it is instructive. The value of the *brochure* is enhanced by an excellent portrait of Mr. Carrodus, as well as of a number of other violin worthies, and the printing, paper, and get up generally are good as could possibly be."—*Musical Answers.*

LONDON :
" STRAD" OFFICE, 3, GREEN TERRACE, ROSEBERY AVENUE, E.C.

"THE STRAD" LIBRARY, No. XIV.

Crown 8vo., Cloth, 2/6, Post Free, 2/9.

SELECTED VIOLIN SOLOS,
AND
HOW TO PLAY THEM,
BY
BASIL ALTHAUS

(Author of " Advice to Pupils and Teachers of the Violin.")

With 283 Musical Examples.

CONTENTS.

INTRODUCTION.

SECTION I.

GRADE A.—Elementary Pieces.
GRADE B.—Easy, not exceeding First Position.
GRADE C.—Easy, using First and Third Position.

SECTION II.

GRADE D.—Moderately Difficult, not exceeding the Third Position.
GRADE E.—Moderately Difficult, as far as the Fifth Position.
GRADE F.—Difficult, especially as regards Sentiment and Expression.

SECTION III.

GRADE G.— Difficult, using all Positions.
GRADE H.—Very Difficult, including Standard Concertos and Concert Pieces.
GRADE I.—For Virtuosi.

LONDON :
" STRAD " OFFICE, 3, GREEN TERRACE, ROSEBERY AVENUE, E.C.

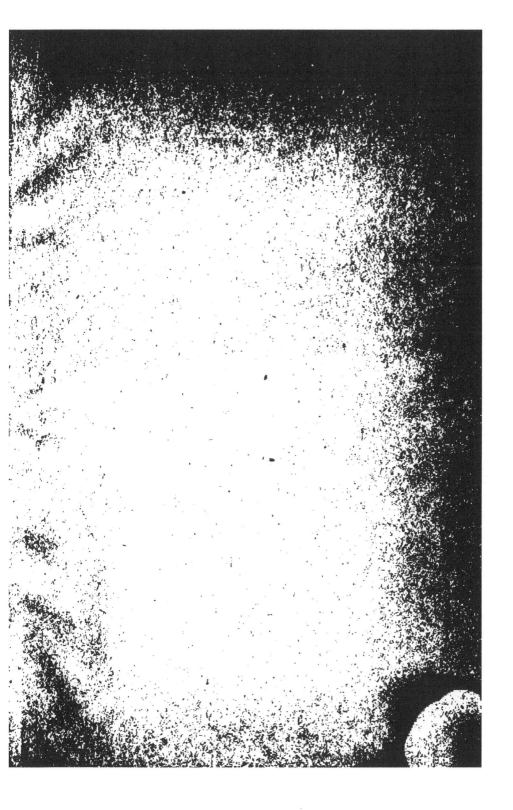

Lightning Source UK Ltd.
Milton Keynes UK
UKOW06n0617210116